English – Ilokano

and

Ilokano – English

Dictionary

– With Some Notes on Ilokano Culture

Daniel H. Wieczorek

English – Ilokano

and

Ilokano – English

Dictionary

– With Some Notes on Ilokano Culture

Daniel H. Wieczorek

ISBN-13: 978-1477522769
ISBN-10: 147752276X

DEDICATION

AND

SINCERE THANKS TO:

ABE; My Language Instructor During Training

RONALD; My Host Brother and Companion During Training

GEORGE; My Best Friend and Companion During my Stay in Gomez

Thank You my Friends!!

English – Ilokano

Ilokano – English

Dictionary

– With Some Notes on Ilokano Culture

TO: The Student of Ilokano;

This English – Ilokano, Ilokano – English Dictionary was prepared by a returned Peace Corps Volunteer, Daniel Wieczorek, in the hopes that it may make your task of learning Ilokano just a little bit easier than it would otherwise be. The words and terms included are those that I had reason to learn in my two years as a Volunteer. I lived and worked in Gomez, Cabbaroguis, Quirino. There was absolutely no English spoken in my barrio and for this reason I had to become as fluent as I could as rapidly as I could if I wanted to be able to converse and be helpful. I had a very good friend who was very patient in explaining new Ilokano terms to me. He helped me right from the start, so when he introduced a new word he would explain its meaning in terms that I already knew.

The first part of this Dictionary is the English – Ilokano portion. You will need to glance briefly at it to see how it is set up. For example; all animals and animal actions are listed under "ANIMALS." All references to birds and bird actions are listed under "BIRDS", all body parts are listed under the heading "BODY & BODY PARTS", and so on. Therefore if you are searching for the Ilokano for the word "head" you will look under the entry "BODY & BODY PARTS" for "BODY – HEAD".

In the Ilokano – English Dictionary the "root words" are underlined. Root words are defined as the word base with no verbal or other affixes[1.]. If you want or need any more information on the Ilokano for a word the root word is what you would look up in your other dictionary. In cases such as "A LA <u>UNA</u>" the underline under <u>UNA</u> indicates that the entire expression "A LA UNA" can be found in the referenced dictionary under UNA. For an entry such as "<u>ADDA</u> <u>KADI</u> <u>SURAT</u> PARA <u>KANIAK</u>?" the underlines indicate that several individual words may be found in the referenced dictionary, but not the entire term. An entry such as "AGPAKLEB (<u>KELLEB</u>)" indicates that the root word for the verb "agpakleb" is kelleb. Note the preponderance of "AG" verbs.

---

1. Root Words are from the: **<u>ILOKO - ENGLISH DICTIONARY</u>**, translated, augmented and revised by Morice Vanoverbergh, C.I.C.M., 1956. This dictionary is available from the "Bishop's House" in Baguio City.

Scientific names are given for most fruits, plants, and trees. These scientific names are also from the referenced dictionary.

I have tried to use examples of most common affixes such as "KA......EN" for superlatives, "MAKA......." indicating an active possibility, "MAKI......" the social affix, "MAIKA......" for numbers, and so on. The "NA" affix usually indicates an adjective, however it may also indicate a past tense usage of an intransitive "MA...." verb.

One particular entry I want to call attention to is "Q., CERTAINLY, WHY NOT?", for which the Ilokano is "HAAN, MAN." It is usually used to answer a negative question, for example you might ask your Ilokano friend "Maybe you <u>don't</u> want to go to town with me?" and your friend will answer "HAAN, MAN." You would literally interpret this as "NO, PLEASE" when in reality your friend is answering "CERTAINLY, WHY NOT?"

Some non-underlined entries can also be found in the referenced dictionary, but with a different meaning. For example, the root word of "MATONGPAL" which is "TONGPAL" is in the referenced dictionary, but the printed definition is exactly the opposite of how "MATONGPAL" was explained to me. This may be an error on my part or it may be an error of the referenced dictionary.

I have strong hopes that this dictionary, my work, will make your work easier. Good Luck and Happy Studying.

One last comment, this dictionary was prepared from a DBASE III+ database. It was sorted (alphabetized) once on the Ilokano, and once on the English, and therefore the entries for both dictionaries are exactly identical, they are merely in a different order.

The "Notes on Ilokano Culture" section was written for a ***University of Alaska - Fairbanks*** class in International Business. This is the reason it sounds rather business oriented.

'Toy gayyem mo,

Daniel H. Wieczorek
P.O. Box 81742
Fairbanks, Alaska 99708
U.S.A.

TABLE OF CONTENTS

SECTION 1
ENGLISH – ILOKANO
DICTIONARY

ENGLISH – ILOKANO DICTIONARY

(ALPHABETIZED ON ENGLISH)

ENGLISH .... **ILOKANO**

A a

able to enter .... makasterick
about, object, purpose .... panggep
absent minded .... talimpungawen
accept, to .... umawat
accompany, to .... agkadua, kumuyog
account, compute, to .... agkuenta
accustom, to .... ruam, maruam
add to .... nayonan
afraid, to be .... mabuteng, agbuteng
again .... manen
agile, nimble .... nasiglat
agree, to .... maibagay
all, total .... amin
allow, to .... ipalubos
alone, solitary, to be .... agmaymaysa
already .... en
also .... met
amaze, to be .... agsiddaaw
and .... ken, ket
angry .... nauyong, naunget
angry, pissed off .... marurud, maassar

ANIMALS

animal- baby chick .... piek
animal- bat, small .... kurarapnit
animal- bull .... bulog
animal- calf .... urbon
animal- castrated .... kapon
animal- cat .... pusa
animal- chew cud, to .... agngatingat
animal- chicken .... manok
animal- chicken feathers or hair .... dutdut

animal- chicken scratching .... karaykayen
animal- chicken wattles .... lambi-lambi
animal- chicken, cackle .... agkotak
animal- chicken, female .... upa
animal- chicken, to mate .... manadaan
animal- clam .... bennek
animal- cocks comb .... tapingar
animal- cow, cattle .... baka
animal- crab .... agatol
animal- crocodile .... buaya
animal- deer .... ugsa
animal- dog .... aso
animal- dog, to bark .... agtaul
animal- dog, to wag tail .... agkalawikiw
animal- duck waddle .... kinni-kinni
animal- duck, brown .... itik
animal- duck, white .... pato
animal- fish, fresh water .... lames
animal- frog general name .... tukak
animal- general term .... animales
animal- goat .... kalding
animal- hatch, egg .... agpessa
animal- horn, antler .... sara
animal- horse .... kabayo
animal- iguana .... banias
animal- leech .... alimatek, alinta
animal- lizard, brown .... alibut
animal- lizard, house .... alutiit
animal- lizard, voice of .... saltek
animal- mouse, rat, shrew .... sangio, bao
animal- mudfish .... dalag
animal- nuang mate, to .... agmaya
animal- pig digging or rooting .... agsubsub
animal- pig, hog .... baboy
animal- pig, to oink .... agungik
animal- piglet .... burias
animal- puppy .... uken
animal- rooster .... kawitan
animal- rooster, to crow .... agtaraok
animal- sheep .... karnero
animal- snail, big, land .... biroroko
animal- snail, edible .... bisukol
animal- snake .... uleg
animal- snake skin (shed) .... lupus
animal- snake, green .... bartin
animal- tadpole .... bayyek
animal- tail .... ipus
animal- tail, no .... kibol, putot
animal- testicles, to remove .... agkapon

animal- to pasture .... agarab, agpastur, agwayway
animal- turkey .... pabo
animal- turtle .... pag-ong
animal- water buffalo .... nuang
animal- wild chicken .... abuyo
animal- wild pig .... alingo
animal- worm .... alumbuyod
animals- back yard .... dingoen
animals- to raise .... agtaraken

another, other .... sabali
answer letter, to .... subalitan
answer, to .... sumungbat
applaud, to .... agpalakpak
arm over shoulder, to put .... agassibay
arrive, to .... sumangpet
as if .... no kas
as, like .... kas
ascend, climb, to .... um-uli, sumang-at
ashes, grey .... dapo
aside from that .... malak-sig iti dayta
Attention! .... Pakdaar!
automobile, car .... kotse
axe blow, glancing, deflected .... sumayag
axle .... ehe

B b

babysit, to .... agawawir
back of something, reverse .... balikid
backwards, to go .... agsanud, tres
bad luck .... malas
bad, evil .... dakes
bag, pouch, purse .... supot
bail out, to .... agkaras
balance, to .... agtimbeng
ball .... bola

BAMBOO

bamboo bomb .... bungbung
bamboo ties .... banban
bamboo- edible shoot .... rabong
bamboo- sharp branches .... pakris
bamboo- varieties .... bayug, bikal, bolo, kawayan kiling

BANANA

banana .... saba
banana bundle .... bulig
banana plantation .... kasabaan
banana sucker .... subbual
banana- dry sheath of leaf .... alupasi
banana- flower, to open .... agoklap
banana- growing together .... siping
banana- hand of bananas .... sapad
banana- sick plantation .... agtungrow
banana- spots on .... gaddil
banana- unopened portion of flower .... sabunganay
banana- varieties .... dippig, lakatan, kanton, guyod, gloria,
.... dato, tumok, seniorita, kamarines,
.... baguio, tondal

baptism .... buniag
barefoot, to go .... agsakasaka
bathe, to .... agdigos
battery .... bateria
Beautiful girl! .... Napintas nga balasang!
beautiful, good looking .... napintas
because .... ngamin
before .... santo, sakanto, sakbay
beg, ask, to .... dumawat
begin, commence, to .... irugi
believe, to .... patien, mamati
between .... nagbaetan
bicycle .... bisikleta
bind or tie, to .... repetten

BIRDS

bird .... billit
bird manure .... lugit
bird trap .... talakob
bird- alight, to .... agdisso
bird- beak of .... sippit
bird- crow .... wak
bird- fly, to .... agtayab
bird- hawk .... sawi, kali
bird- kingfisher .... salaksak
bird- night .... saksakulap
bird- night hawk .... kulipato
bird- nuang .... korkoridong

bird- oriole .... kiaw
bird- owl .... puek
bird- pigeon .... kalapati
bird- small, grey color .... panal
bird- small, hawklike .... kongkong, mangabuyo
bird- swallow .... sallapingaw
bird- white breast, black beak .... gikgik
bird- wing .... payak

birthday .... pinnakaeanak
black magic, to practice .... manggagamud
blacker & blacker .... ngumisngisit nga ngumisngisit
blame, to shift .... agpatodon
blanket .... ules
blister, burn, to (sunburn) .... aglapitog
blow horn, to .... agbusina
blow on, to .... agpuyot
blow pipe .... anguyob
board .... tabla
boat, small .... banka

BODY FUNCTIONS

body fnc.- awake, to .... agriing
body fnc.- be born, to .... aganak
body fnc.- blind, sun .... masisirap
body fnc.- blink eyes, to .... agkirem
body fnc.- blow nose, to .... agpangres
body fnc.- bowels, to move .... tumakki
body fnc.- breathe hard, to .... agal-al
body fnc.- burp, to .... agtig-ab
body fnc.- chew, to .... agngalngal, karat-om
body fnc.- clear throat, to .... agseg-am
body fnc.- cold, to have a .... agpanateng
body fnc.- conceive child, to .... agnginaw
body fnc.- cough, to .... aguyek
body fnc.- crack knuckles, to .... agrittok
body fnc.- diarrhea, to have .... agburis
body fnc.- dream, to .... agtagainep
body fnc.- eyes, to close .... agkidem
body fnc.- fart, to .... umottot
body fnc.- footstep, pace .... addang
body fnc.- gargle, to .... agmulumog
body fnc.- haircut, to have .... agpukis
body fnc.- hiccough, to .... agsaiddek
body fnc.- horny, to be .... agottog
body fnc.- laugh, to .... agkatawa

body fnc.- masturbate, to .... agsalsal, isalsal
body fnc.- nosebleed, to .... agdaringongo
body fnc.- pregnant, to be .... masikog
body fnc.- rise, to get up .... bumangon
body fnc.- shave, to .... agkiskis
body fnc.- shiver, to .... agtigariger
body fnc.- short rest, to take a .... aginana
body fnc.- sleep, to .... maturog
body fnc.- sleep, to pretend, He is .... Aginturturog-na
body fnc.- smile, to .... agisem
body fnc.- sneeze, to .... agbaen
body fnc.- sniff, to .... agsinglut
body fnc.- snore, to .... agorok
body fnc.- spit, to .... agtopra
body fnc.- stomach growl, to .... aggaradugud
body fnc.- stretch, to-upon waking .... aginat
body fnc.- suck, baby bottle, etc. .... agammol
body fnc.- swallow, sound of .... agkanaldook
body fnc.- swallow, to .... tilmunen
body fnc.- sweat, to .... agling-et
body fnc.- tap fingers, to .... agdallapeg
body fnc.- urinate, to .... umisbo
body fnc.- voice .... timek, uni
body fnc.- vomit, to .... agsarua
body fnc.- weep, cry, to .... agsangit, aglua
body fnc.- yawn, to .... agsuyaab

BODY & BODY PARTS

body .... bagi
body odor .... anglit
body- afterbirth .... kadkadua
body- ankle .... gorong
body- ankle bone .... lipay-lipay
body- anus .... kuriit
body- armpit .... kili-kili
body- athletes foot, to have .... agtarindanum
body- back .... bukot, likod
body- back bone .... dori-dori
body- beard .... barbas
body- blind .... bulag
body- blister .... kapuyo
body- blood .... dara
body- bone .... tulang
body- brain .... utek
body- breast .... soso
body- breath .... sang-aw
body- buttocks .... ubet

body- a callus .... lalat, callio
body- Can you smell me? .... Mabalin nga ma-angot-nak?
body- cheeks .... ping-ping
body- chest .... barukong
body- chin .... timid
body- circumcise, to .... agkogit
body- clitoris .... mani-mani
body- cold, to feel .... malammin
body- cut, bloody .... sugat
body- dandruff .... lasi
body- deaf .... tuleng
body- dislocated body part .... nablo (bollo)
body- drown, to .... malmes (lemmes)
body- ear, lobe of .... piditpidit
body- ears .... lapayag
body- elbow .... siko
body- erection .... imptog
body- eye, mote in the .... puling
body- eyebrow .... kiday-kiday
body- eyelash .... kurimatmat
body- eyes .... mata
body- face, similar .... kaingingas
body- face, the .... rupa
body- feet, tired .... napakil ti saka
body- fingernail .... koko
body- fingers .... ramay
body- flesh .... lasag
body- foot .... saka
body- foot asleep .... napipikel ti saka
body- foot, sole of .... dapan
body- forehead .... muging
body- getting fatter .... lumuklukmeg
body- getting thinner .... kumotkottong
body- goose bumps .... sungar
body- hair, curly .... kulot
body- hair, feathers .... dutdut
body- hair, grey .... uban
body- hair, no .... kalbo
body- hair, of the head .... bo-ok
body- hair, pubic .... urmot
body- hair, whorl in the .... alipuspus
body- hand .... ima
body- head .... ulo
body- head, back of .... teltel
body- healthy .... nasalun-at, nakaradkad
body- heart .... puso
body- heel (of foot) .... mukod
body- hips .... siket
body- hot, being .... nasalimuot

body- I have a headache. .... Nasakit ti ulok.
body- intestine, guts.......... bagis
body- knee .... tumeng
body- knuckle (or bamboo knuckle).......... boko
body- leg, calf of .... bugi
body- lips .... bibig
body- liver .... dalem
body- lymph gland .... salsalamagi
body- mole, birthmark.......... siding
body- mouth.......... ngiwat
body- muscles, sore.......... naktang
body- mute.......... umel
body- My mind hurts. .... Nasakit ti panunot ko.
body- My stomach hurts. .... Nasakit ti buksit ko.
body- naked .... lamolamo, silalabus
body- navel.......... puseg
body- neck .... tengnged
body- nipple .... mungay
body- nose .... agong
body- one-eyed .... bulding
body- palm of hand .... dakulap
body- penis .... buto
body- penis, shaft of .... lateg
body- penis, to move in erection.......... agkinod
body- pimple.......... kamoro
body- pus .... nana
body- ribs.......... paragpag
body- scab .... keggang
body- scar.......... piglat
body- sexual intercourse, to have .... agyut
body- shoulder.......... abaga
body- sickness return, relapse .... nabegnat
body- side of the .... bakrang
body- skin .... kudil
body- skin, covered.......... maabungan
body- skin, slice off a piece of.......... matikapan
body- skin, white spots on .... kamanaw
body- smegma .... kaper
body- smell, bad.......... naangdod
body- smooth skin .... nalabudoy
body- soul .... karma
body- sperm.......... kissit
body- sting, to, the skin.......... naapges
body- stomach .... buksit, tian
body- tears.......... lua
body- teeth.......... ngipen
body- teeth to be loose.......... agwaliwali
body- temple of head .... pispis
body- testicles.......... ukel-ukel

body- thigh.......luppo
body- throat.......karabukob
body- toes.......ramay nga saka
body- tongue.......dila
body- upper arm.......takiag
body- vagina.......oki
body- veins.......urat
body- vulva.......kibong-kibong
body- wrist.......pongopongoan

boil vegetables or meat, to.......aglambong
boil, eggs, to.......ilingta
boil, to.......maburek, ipaburek
bolo, machete.......buneng
bolt.......turnilyo
bone, crushed.......manarnar
book.......libro
bored, weary, to be.......mauma
borrow, to.......bumulod
bottle.......botelia
bottle cap.......tonsan
boundary.......kategan
box, case.......kaha, kahon
brag, to.......naparayag, agpalastog
bran.......tuyo
branch, new.......saringit
bread.......tinapay
break eggs, glass.......naboong
bribe, to.......pasuksuk
bridge.......rangtay
bring, to.......itugot
broke, snapped, trees bones, etc.......natokkol
broken or rolling ground.......likkalikkaong
broom, indoor.......walis
broom, outdoor.......kaykay
bucket, pail.......timba
bulb, flashlight, etc.......bumbilia
bullet.......bala
bump head, to.......maitomeg
bump, a.......dugul
buneng, back of.......bangad
buneng, pencil, point of.......tirad
buneng, sheath for.......kaluban
buneng, turned edge.......mateptep
burn bad.......nakusep
burn good.......narubrub
burn yourself, to.......agsinit
burn, pile & burn brush.......aginson

burn, scorch, forest fire, to.......agpuor, mapuor
burned food.......nakset (kesset), nasinit
but.......ngem
butcher, to.......agparti
button.......botonis
buy, purchase, to.......gumatang

C c

calendar.......kalenderio
can, tin.......lata
candle.......kandela
candy, coconut balls.......bokayo
candy, flat coconut.......bukarelyo
candy, sugar cane.......tagapulut
cant (squared timber).......tablon
cant hook.......kamsut
carbide.......kalburo
care, concern.......biang
careful, cautious, to be.......agannad
carry cargo for somebody, to.......agkaryada
carry on head, to.......agsosoon
carry on shoulder, to.......agbaklay
carry to somebody, to.......ipawit
carry, to.......agawit, agbunag
carry, to (crossed items).......pagkinorosen
carry, to (parallel items).......pagornosen
catch something thrown, to.......agsippaw
catch up with, to.......umabut
catch, to (like a chicken).......agtiliw
certainly, of course.......siempre
central, center.......sentro
chain.......kawar
chain saw, to use.......agtestes
chalk line.......paltik (littik)
change, relieve, replace, to.......masukat
Changes light to night (dusk).......Aginagaw ti sipnget ken lawag.
charcoal.......uging, uring
charcoal pile.......pugon
chase, to.......agkamat
cheat, to.......agsaur
cheese.......kuesa
chew betel nut, to.......agmama
chicken, crack in tail, breach.......giwang
chili pepper.......sili
chock wheel, to.......ikelso
choose, select, to.......mapili
chop, to.......agbalsig, balsigen

chopping block .... langdet
church .... simbaan
cigarette .... sigarilio
cigarette, to light from another .... agsendi
cigarette, to put out .... agrungrung
clean .... nadalus
clean with fingers (ear, nose) .... agkutikut
clean, bamboo knuckles, to .... agsalingsing
clean, grass, etc, to .... agwagwag
clear, light, bright .... nalawag
cliff .... tipang
clock or watch .... relos
close door, window .... irikep
close, near, like friends .... nadikket
close, shut, to .... serraan
closer, move to .... agsedsed, agdidikket
cloth, piece of, or rag .... nisnis
cloth, rag .... lupot

CLOTHING

clothes .... bado
clothes- belt .... sentrom
clothes- boots .... buta
clothes- gloves .... guantis
clothes- handkerchief .... panio
clothes- hat .... kallogong
clothes- headband .... baridbid
clothes- hole in .... butbut
clothes- pants, trousers .... pantalon
clothes- rain coat .... kapote
clothes- shoes .... sapatos
clothes- shoes, to lace .... agkordon
clothes- sleeveless sweater .... tsleko
clothes- slippers, step-ins .... tsinela
clothes- socks .... medias
clothes- to rinse .... igawgaw
clothes- wear, to .... agbado, isuout

cloud .... ulep
coconut husk floor polisher .... lumpaso
coffee .... kapi
coffee maker, teapot .... kapateria
coffin .... longon
cold, frigid, icy, water, food .... nalamiis
cold, frigid, temperature .... nalam-ek
collect debt, to .... agsingir
collide, strike, bump, to .... matim-og

COLORS

color- able to change .... burik
color- black .... nangisit
color- blue .... azul
color- brown .... tsokolate
color- green .... berde
color- orange .... orens
color- red .... nalabaga
color- white .... napudaw, puraw
color- yellow .... duyaw

comb .... sagaysay
come, to .... umay
common, widespread .... sapasap
compete, contest, to .... agsasalisal
connector word .... nga
consistent, chewy, firm .... nakilnet
construct, to (house, building) .... agpatakder
contagious .... makaalis
continue, to .... maituluy
cook, to .... agluto
corn, ear of w/ corn removed .... rubu
corn, few kernels on cob .... bungal
corn, to shell .... agpusi, mapusi
corn, to shell w/ nail & board .... aggadgad
corner .... soli
correct, right .... husto
cotton .... kapas
count, to .... bilangen
cover up, to .... agakkub
crack in board .... mabistak
crack, in glass .... gettang
crack, small, in board .... birri
cracked earth .... narengngat ti daga
crazy .... bagtit
creek, brook .... waig
crossing, junction .... nagsabatan
crumbs .... marigmig
crush, to .... maipit, nalipit
culvert .... imburnal
cut up, to .... pisien, iwaiwa

D d

dainty eater .... nakusim
dam, levee, dike .... tambak
Damn it! .... Okinnana!
dance, to .... agsala
dark .... nasipnget
debt, liability .... utang
delay, detain, to .... agtaktak
delicate, fragile, weak, brittle .... narukop
delicious .... naimas
descend, to .... bumaba, umulog, sumalog
dessert, to .... panawan
destination .... destinio
destroy or ruin, to .... agrakrak
destroyed .... naperde
devil .... diablo
dew .... amor, linnaaw
die, to .... matay
difference .... dipperentia
difficult .... narigat
dig a hole, to .... ikali, agkali
dim .... naridem, nakudrep
dip (like bread in coffee) .... isawsaw

DIRECTIONS

direction- north .... amianan
direction- south .... abagatan
direction- east .... daya
direction- west .... laud
direction- right .... kanawan
direction- left .... kanigid
direction- straight ahead .... diretso
direction- (What direction?) .... banda (Ania ti banda?)

dirt, clump of .... bingkol
dirt, soil, earth .... daga
dirt, to cover with .... aggabor, magaboran
dirty, filthy .... narugit
disagree, to .... agsinabali
disappear, lose, to .... napukaw, maawan
disappear, to .... umawanawan
disappointed, to be .... maikapis
dizzy, to be .... maulaw
do, make, build, to .... agaramid
doubt, adverb implying .... sa

dried .... nagango
drink, to .... uminom
drip, trickle, leak, to .... agtedted
drizzle, to .... agarbis
drunk .... nabartek
dry .... namaga
dry season .... agigaaw
dry, to .... aggango
durable .... nalagda
dusty .... natapok
dwell, to .... agyan
dwelling place .... pagigyanan
dying, death struggle .... agbugsut

E e

each & every one .... tunggal maysa
earnings .... tangdan
earthquake .... gingined
easy, cheap .... nalaka
eat raw, to .... kilawen
eat sugar cane, to .... agusus
eat with hands, to .... agkamet
eat, to .... mangan (kaan)
edge, margin .... igid
egg .... itlog
election .... eleksion
electricity, current .... kurente
emerge, issue forth, go out, to .... rumuar
empty, ears of grain, seeds .... eppes
empty, to .... ipattog
enemy .... kabosor, kasuron, kagurra
engine, machine .... makina
enough, stop .... basta, huston
enter, go in, to .... umuneg, sumrek (serrek)
envelope .... sobre ti surat
errand, to go on .... baonen
especially .... nongrona
even (versus odd), equal .... paris
Even I also. .... Uray siak met.
even, also .... uray
excessive .... nalabes
expensive, dear .... nangina
expert, efficient, capable .... nalaing
explode, to .... bumtak (bettak)
expose oneself to the wind, to .... agberber
extinguish, to .... iddepen
extra .... sobra

extra, additional .... taraudi
extract oil, to .... agsinglag
eye glasses .... anchokos

F f

fall apart, book, clothes .... napigis
fall down, drop .... natulid, natinnag
family .... pfamilia
famine, time of scarcity .... gawat
far, distant .... adayo
fare (for the ride) .... plete
farm, the (place to plant) .... uma, pagmulaan
farm, upland .... bangkag
fat, fleshy .... nalukmeg
fatty, oily, greasy .... nataba
favorite, most desirable .... paborita
feast, Christmas, Easter .... Paskua
fence, hedge .... alad
fertilize, to .... agabuno
fight, to .... aglaban, agdanog
fight, to (with buneng) .... tumagbat
fill, a crack, to .... agsingat
fill, to .... mapunno
fingernail, to break .... malsiyeb
finish, to (work, etc) .... malpas (leppas)
finished, ended (month, year, etc) .... natapos
fire .... apuy
fire, place to make .... pagarunan
fire, to light .... agarun, agapuy
firecracker .... labintador
fish sauce, watery .... patis
fish sauce .... boggoong
fish with hands, to .... agkammel, agkalap
fish with rod, to .... agliwliw
fish, small dried .... galunggung
fishpond .... tanggal, pupukan
flag .... bandera
flexible .... nalap-it
flip over, to .... agtiritir
float in, to .... maianud
float, to .... tumpaw (tapaw)
flood, to .... aglayos
flow, sap .... nagbusingar, agtutot
fold cloth, to .... kopinen
fold in half, to .... piliquen
follow, to .... sumaruno, suroten, sumurot

food settle (in stomach), to .... agpalpa
food, other than rice .... sida
food, to give to (to feed) .... pakanen (kaan)
for example .... no kaspangarigan
for sure .... segurado
for .... para
force, coerce, to .... mapilit
forest .... bakir
forget, to .... malipatan
forgive, pardon, to .... pakawanen
fragile, dangerous .... delikado
fray, to .... agsisir
free, no charge .... libre
fresh, meat, fish, etc .... nasadiwa
friendly .... manakigayyem
from (place) .... aggapo
from before .... dati, gagangay, latta, sigud
from, time or place .... manipud (sipud)
front, forepart .... sango

FRUITS

fruit .... bunga
fruit- bok choy .... pitsay
fruit- cabbage .... repolyo
fruit- carrot .... karot
fruit- cucumber .... pepino
fruit- flesh of .... gunnot
fruit- guava .... bayabas
fruit- jack *(Artocarpus integrifolia)* .... langka
fruit- like a cucumber *(Luffa cylindrica)* .... kabatiti
fruit- papaya *(Carica papaya)* .... papaya
fruit- pineapple .... pinia
fruit- pomelo *(Citrus decumana)* .... lukban
fruit- radish .... rabanos
fruit- rattan *(Calamus sp.)* .... littoko
fruit- small .... busel
fruit- starfruit *(Averrhoa carambola)* .... daldaligan
fruit- sweetsop *(Arnona squamosa)* .... atis
fruit- tomato .... kamatis
fruit- watermelon .... sandia
fruits- ridges on .... bilid

frustrated .... napaay
fry, to .... iprito
fuel wood .... sungrod
funeral .... ponpon

funnel .... imbudo

G g

g-string .... baag
garden, to .... aghardin
general term for anything .... kua
get, to .... alaen
ghost .... al-alia
giant .... hegante
gift from the city .... pasalubong
gift .... regalo
give, to .... ited
glutton, good eater .... narawet
go around in circles, to .... agrikrikos, agliklikaw
go, to .... mapan, in
God .... Dios
gold .... balitok
gong .... gansa
gong, to .... agbatangtang
Good afternoon to you. (sing) .... Naimbag nga malem mo.
good grass, new growth .... naraber
good luck .... nagasat, swerte
Good morning to you. (sing) .... Naimbag nga bigat mo.
Good night to you. (sing) .... Naimbag nga rabii-m.
Good noontime to you. (pl) .... Naimbag nga aldaw yo amin.
good, well .... naimbag, nasayaat, mayat
grass to cut by holding it .... pinelas, pinesat, ginapas

GRASSES

grass- a weed .... payokpok
grass- bamboo *(Miscanthus sinensis)* .... runo
grass- coarse, tall *(Saccharum spontaneum)* .... lidda
grass- cogon *(Imperata cylindrica)* .... pan-aw
grass- the sharp kind .... alladan
grass- to cut .... agtabas, agsiprau
grass- to trim .... agsipsip
grass- yard *(Eleusine indica)* .... gagabuten

greet, welcome, to .... agkablaaw, kumablaaw
grow, to .... agtubo
grows fast .... napartak nga agtubo
guard, watch, to .... agbantay
guitar, sound of .... agkutengteng
gun, bamboo .... palsuut

gun, rifle .... paltog

H h

habit .... ugali
haggle or bargain, to .... agud-ud, tumawar
handsome .... naguapo, nataer, nataraki
hang by neck, to .... agbekkel
hang, to (on back of jeepney) .... agbitin
happen, occur, to .... mapasamak
Happy New Year to you all. .... Naragsak nga baru nga tawen yo.
Happy trip! .... Naragsak nga pinagbiahe-mo!
happy, joyous .... naragsak
hard, solid, firm .... natangken
harrow, to .... agsagad
harvest anything, to .... agpurus
harvest bananas, to .... agtebba
harvest by cutting stem, to .... agpolting
harvest rice, to .... aggapas
harvest rice, to (by hand) .... agani
harvest, pick fruits, to .... agapit, agburas
he, she, it .... isu, isuna
heaven, sky, paradise .... langit
heavy .... nadagsen
help each other, to .... agtinnulong
help, to .... tumulong
here - near speaker .... ditoy
hide or conceal, to .... aglemmeng, sumoksok, aglinged
high, lofty .... nangato, ngato
highway .... espeltado
hill .... turod
hold at armslength, to .... agtapaya
hold, to .... agiggam
hole .... abut
hole, for axle .... abbutaw
holes in road, field, etc .... likkaong
holler or call, to .... agpukkaw, ayaban
home, to take home .... iawid
honey .... diro
honorific, ma'am .... manang
honorific, sir .... manong
honor, to .... dayawen
hook .... kawit
hope .... barbareng, sapay la koma
hot, heat (weather) .... napudot
hot, red .... nabara
hot, spicy .... nagasang, naadat
hot, sultry, humid .... nadagaang

HOUSE ITEMS

house .... balay
house post .... adigi
house- addition to .... taguab
house- basket with handles .... labba
house- bathroom .... kasilias
house- bed .... katre
house- bench, chair .... tugaw, bangko
house- bowl .... mallokong
house- collapse .... marba (rebba), marpuog (reppoog)
house- dipper (for liquids) .... sartin
house- door .... ridaw
house- eaves of .... sagumaymay
house- floor .... datar
house- foot locker .... lakasa
house- gable end of .... bayangbayang
house- glass, drinking .... baso
house- hearth, stove .... dalikan
house- kitchen .... kosina
house- ladle .... aklo
house- peak of .... bobongan
house- plate .... pinggan
house- porch, balcony .... balkon
house- roof .... atep
house- roof, cross pieces .... sigpit
house- roof, rafter .... pasanggir
house- roofing, tin .... yero, galva
house- room .... kuarto
house- spoon .... kutsara
house- table .... lamisaan
house- tablefork .... tenidor
house- to build a .... agbalay
house- wall .... diding
house- wall header .... awanan
house- window .... tawa
house- wok .... pariok

hurry, to .... agdaras, darasen
husk, to .... agukis, buksilan
hut, rest .... kalapaw
hypocotyl, seedling .... rusing

I i

I am able to be patient. .... Makaananos-ak.
I am full. (of food) .... Nabsog-ak (bussog).
I am happy if I am with you. .... Naragsak-ak no agkadua-ta.
I am hungry. .... Mabisin-ak.
I am joking. .... Agang angaw-ak.
I am only passing. .... Lumabas-ak laeng.
I am sorry (to you). .... Pasinsiya-(ka).
I don't know. .... Diak ammo. Madik ammo.
I don't remember. .... Diak malagip. Madik malagip.
I don't want (like). .... Diak kayat. Haan ko nga kayat.
I feel bad. .... Madi ti riknak.
I feel like sleeping. .... Makaturturog-ak.
I forgot. .... Nalipat-ak.
I have no time. .... Awan oras ko.
I have nothing to do. .... Awan ti aramidek.
I have something to say to you. .... Adda ti ibagak kenka.
I have something to show you. .... Adda ti ipakitak kenka.
I hope so. .... Sapay la koma.
I just ate. .... Kapangpangan-ko.
I like, want. .... Kayat ko.
I love you. (sing) .... Ayayat-enka.
I miss you. (sing) .... Mailiiliwak kenka.
I received your letter. .... Naawat ko ti surat mo.
I will come home soon. .... Agawid-ak to.
I will take that home. .... Iawid-ko dayta.
I will try my best. .... Padasek ti kabaelak.
I'll be the one! .... Siak-on!
I, me .... ak, siak

ice .... yelo
if .... no
immediately .... dagus
important .... importante
incline or bend the head, to .... agdumug
indian giver .... babawi
industrious .... nagaget
ingredients .... rekado
invitation .... imbitar

INSECTS

insect- ant lion .... taptapuyo
insect- ant, black .... antutungal
insect- ant, general term .... koton

insect- ant, red .... aboos
insect- aphid .... aplat
insect- bee, small .... alig
insect- beetle, click .... kittool
insect- beetle, green & violet .... sammisammi
insect- beetle, june .... abal-abal
insect- beetle, red & black .... baka-baka
insect- beetle, rice .... buk-buk
insect- bite, to mosquitoes, etc. .... kumagat
insect- butterfly .... kulibangbang
insect- caterpillar .... budwa-budwan
insect- centipede .... gayaman
insect- cicada .... kundidit
insect- cicada, big (male) .... riari
insect- cockroach .... ipes
insect- coconut beetle .... barrairong
insect- cricket .... kuriat
insect- dragon fly .... tuwato
insect- firefly .... kulalanti
insect- flea .... timel
insect- general term .... insekto
insect- grasshopper .... dudon
insect- head louse .... koto
insect- house fly .... ngilaw
insect- itchy hairs of caterpillar .... budo
insect- millipede .... diken-diken
insect- mole cricket .... ararawan
insect- mosquito .... lamok
insect- mosquito net .... moskitero
insect- praying mantis .... wasay-wasay
insect- scorpion .... manggagama
insect- small biting fly .... sepsep
insect- spider .... lawwa-lawwa
insect- spider web .... saput
insect- sting, to (bee sting) .... agsilud
insect- stink bug .... dangaw
insect- termite .... anay
insect- termite, flying stage .... simut-simut
insect- wasp .... alumpipinig
insect- wasp, bumblebee .... alimbubuyog
insect- wasp, mud .... akut-akut
insect- wasp, yellow jacket .... ayukan
insect- worms in fruits .... igges

iron .... landok
itchy .... nagatel, nabudo, naariek

J j

jar .... garapon
jealous, for things .... umapal
jealous, for wife .... agimun
join two items, lengthen .... isilpo
jump, to .... lumagto
just left (he/she) .... kaapapan-(na)

K k

kettle .... kaldero
key .... tolbek
kick, to .... kumugtar
kill time, to .... agpalennek
kill, to .... pinnatay
kind, type, species .... klasse
knife .... kumpit, kutsilio
knife- dull .... nangudel
knife- pocket .... lansita
knife- rice .... kumpay
knife- sharp .... natadem
knife- small nick in blade .... gusing
knock, to .... agkakok
knot .... siglut
know, to .... ammo

L l

ladder .... agdan
large, big .... dakkel
last, latest .... naudi
lasting, enduring, untiring .... napaut
lateral shoot, tine, point .... sanga
law, rule .... linteg
lazy .... nasadut
lazy, always .... sinulit, sinadut
lead, to lead by the reins .... ukoden
leaf, (plant, book, etc.) .... bulong
leaf, central vein .... iit
leak, to .... agobo
lean, to .... agirig
leaning, unequal .... bangking
learn, to .... agsuro, isuro
leave secretly, escape, to .... aglibas
leave, to run away .... pumanaw, agtalaw
leaves or shoots, young .... uggot

lend, to .... ipabulod
Let's go together. (sing) .... Maki-kuyog-ta.
Let's rejoice. (pl) .... Agragsak-tayo.
Let's work together. (sing) .... Makitrabaho-ta.
letter, alphabetic character .... letra
lick, to .... agdilpat, dilapen
lie down together, to .... maki-idda
lie down, to .... agidda
lie on back, to .... agdata
lie on side, to .... agsikig
lie on stomach, to .... agpakleb (kelleb)
lie, fib, to .... aglastog, bulataw
lift kamote vine, to .... bagoten
lift, to .... agbagkat
light .... silaw
light a lamp, to .... agsinga
light weight .... nalag-an
lightning .... kimat
like that .... bakano, kasdiay, kasta
like this .... kastoy
Little by little., Slow by slow. .... Saga bassit.
live (alive) .... agbiag, mabiag
lock the door, to .... ikandado, makatolbek
lodging place .... pagdagusen
lonely, lonesome .... talipungawen
long .... atiddog
look behind, backwards, to .... agtaliaw, tumaliaw
look down, to .... agtan-aw, tuman-aw
loose .... nalokay
lose, to, or be defeated .... maabak
lunch, provisions .... balun

M m

mail, to .... agibuson
manure, dung, excrement .... takki
many .... adu
many many .... grabi
many times .... adu nga daras
map .... mapa
marble .... hulin
marbles, to shoot .... mapitik
market .... tiendaan, palengke
matches .... gorabis
material wealth .... nasanikua
maybe, probably .... seguru
measles .... kamoras

MEASURE

measure- 75 liters .... kaban
measure- half way .... medyo
measure- one foot .... pea
measure- one-fourth (1/4) .... kakapat
measure- one-half (1/2) .... kaguddua
measure- three liters .... salup

meat .... karne
meat, cooked in blood .... dinardaraan
meat, tender soft .... nalumoy
meat, tough .... nakulbet
medicine .... agas
meet, to .... agsabet, sumabet
melt, to .... marunaw
Merry Christmas to you all. .... Naimbag nga Paskua yo amin.
mildew .... ratik
milk .... gatas
milk, coconut .... gata, getta
mirror, glass .... sarming
mix, to .... pagampuren
mold .... boot

MONEY

money .... kuarta
money- 25 cent piece .... binting
money- 50 cent piece .... salapi
money- coins .... barya
money- to change .... suplian

moon, full .... kabus
moon, new .... linnid
more .... ad-adu
moss .... lumot

SUPERLATIVES

most- best friend .... kadikketen nga gayyem
most- biggest .... kadakkelen
most- hardest .... katangkenen
most- most beautiful .... kapintasen
most- most difficult .... karegaten
most- smallest .... kabassiten

motorcycle .... motorsiklo
mountain .... bantay
move, change residence .... umalis, umakar
move, stir, to .... agkuti
mud, stuck in the .... nailubo, nabalahoo
muddy .... napitak, nalubo, nalutlut
municipality, part of .... baranggay

N n

nails, to drive .... ipalpal
name .... nagan
name, family .... apalido
narrow .... akikid
near .... asideg
nearly, almost .... dandani, nganngani, nagistayan
necklace, rosary .... kuentas
need, necessary .... masapul
needle .... dagum
Never mind! .... Haan nga bale!
news .... damag
no .... saan, haan, madi
no holes .... nalimpia
no more .... naibus
No problem. .... Awan problema.
no steepness, level, equal .... napatad
noisy, irritating .... naringgor
noisy, say many times .... nariri
None of your business. .... Awan ti biang mo.
Not even one. .... Awan uray maysa.
Not really. .... Paltos.
not scared, brave, bold .... natured
not, not to like .... madi

NUANG

nuang calf- male .... kalakyan
nuang cart- box on .... kasig
nuang cart- cross pieces .... surelas
nuang cart- harness .... batikola
nuang cart- harness, back piece .... abukot, barangawid
nuang cart- long sticks on .... pallatiwan
nuang cart- wood for axle .... kulba
nuang rub against tree, etc. .... aggidigid
nuang wallow .... lubnak

nuang- brush against something .... pumanakpak
nuang- cart for cant .... dalayday
nuang- notches on yoke .... getget
nuang- rash from riding wet .... rarasa
nuang- reins .... padno
nuang- rope around horns .... paulo
nuang- rope for pasturing .... wayway
nuang- rope for plowing .... pamitik, guyodan
nuang- shake flies off, to .... agabug
nuang- short rope for yoke .... kalombida
nuang- to move .... iyakar
nuang- to stimulate milk supply .... agtonged
nuang- voice of .... agngoak
nuang- wag tail .... agsaplit
nuang- wiggle ears, to .... agpayapay
nuang- yoke for .... pako, sangol
nuangs to fight, butt heads .... agsangdo

NUMBERS

number- general term .... numero
number- one .... maysa, una (Sp.)
number- two .... dua, dos (Sp.)
number- three .... tallo, tres (Sp.)
number- four .... uppat, kuatro (Sp.)
number- five .... lima, sinko (Sp.)
number- six .... innem, seis (Sp.)
number- seven .... pito, siete (Sp.)
number- eight .... walo, otso (Sp.)
number- nine .... siam, nuebe (Sp.)
number- ten .... sangapulo, djis (Sp.)
number- eleven .... sangapulo ket maysa, onse (Sp.)
number- twelve .... sangapulo ket dua, dose (Sp.)
number- twenty .... dua pulo, biente (Sp.)
number- thirty .... tallo pulo, triente (Sp.)
number- one-hundred .... sangagasut
number- one-thousand .... sangaribu
number- first .... umuna
number- second .... maikadua
number- third .... maikatlo
number- fourth .... maikauppat
number- One more please. .... Maysa pay man.

nut (for bolt) .... roskas

O o

odd (versus even) .... salaisi
oil, coconut .... lana
oil, lard .... manteka
Okay then. .... Sige ngarud.
old, stale .... daan
one by one .... sagaysan
only .... laeng
open .... lukatan
open, to (flower) .... agokrad
or, lest .... wenno
overcast .... alibuyong
overtake & pass .... lumumba

OWN

own- I own .... Kukuak
own- You own (sing) .... Kukuam
own- He, She, It owns .... Kukuana
own- We (2) own .... Kukuata
own- We (exclusive) own .... Kukuami
own- We (inclusive) own .... Kukuatayo
own- You (pl) own .... Kukuakayo
own- They own .... Kukuada
own- Who owns that? .... Sino makin kukua dayta?

P p

pack (dirt), to .... agpayat
paint, to .... agpintar
palms, to read .... agpalad
paper .... papel
paper, toilet .... pagilo
pass under something, to .... osoken
patient, to be .... aganos
pay, to .... agbayad
peaceful, quiet, calm .... natalna
peel, leaves, like onion .... lip-ak

PEOPLE

people- bachelor, new .... baru
people- bisexual .... silahis
people- bride .... trahe
people- brother, sister .... kabsat

people- brother-in-law .... bayaw
people- child .... anak
people- child, baby .... ubing
people- Chinese person .... insik
people- companion .... kadua
people- cousin .... kasinsin
people- elder brother or sister .... kaka
people- father, dad .... tatang
people- father, priest .... padi
people- friend .... gayyem
people- friended .... nagayyem
people- girl friend .... nubia
people- grandparent .... apo
people- groom .... barong
people- homosexual .... bakla
people- human being .... tao
people- man, male .... lalaki
people- man, old .... lakay
people- mother .... nanang
people- neighbor .... kaaroba
people- relatives .... kabagian
people- wife, husband, mate .... asawa
people- woman, female .... babai
people- woman, old .... baket
people- woman, single, unmarried .... balasang
people- younger brother or sister .... adi
people- visitor .... bisita

perhaps, maybe, wonder .... ngata
persuade to come .... awisen
pet, to .... agapros
photo .... letrato
pick up, to .... agpidut
pile .... nabunton
pile, make a big (overburden) .... agsalensen
pile, to make .... agkamada
pillow, cushion .... pungan
pillowcase .... supot nga pungan
pinch fingers under (heavy) .... malipit
pinch, to .... agkidel
pitiful, woeful .... kakaasi
place, spot .... lugar
plant, to .... agmula, imula

PLANTS

plant- 6' tall, big long leaves .... banay
plant- amaranth *(Amaranthus viridis)* .... kuantong
plant- bean *(Dolichos ablab)* .... parda
plant- bean, cowpea, yardlong *(Vigna sinensis)* .... otong
plant- bean, lima *(Phaseolus lunatus)* .... patani
plant- bean, mungo *(Phaseolus radiatus)* .... balatong
plant- bean, tree *(Pithecolobium dulce)* .... damortis
plant- bean, winged *(Psophocarpus spp.)* .... pallang
plant- bean, yambean *(Pachyrhizus erosus)* .... sinkamas
plant- betel pepper *(Ehretia navesii)* .... gawed
plant- bittermelon *(Momordica charantia)* .... paria
plant- corn .... mais
plant- edible *(Tacca palmata)* .... tigi
plant- edible tubers *(Dioscorea fasciculata)* .... tugi
plant- eggplant *(Solanum melongena)* .... tarong
plant- flower .... sabung
plant- garlic *(Allium sativum)* .... bawang
plant- ginger *(Zingiber officinale)* .... laya
plant- jute *(Corchorus olitorius)* .... saluyot
plant- mushroom .... oong
plant- onion *(Allium cepa)* .... lasona
plant- pea, pigeon *(Cajanus cajan)* .... kardis
plant- peanut *(Arachis hypogeia)* .... mani
plant- rattan *(Calamus spp.)* .... way
plant- root of .... ramot
plant- sensitive *(Mimosa pudica)* .... babain
plant- smelly *(Hyptis suaveolens)* .... bangbangsit
plant- squash .... karabasa
plant- squash, bottle guord *(Lagenaria leucantha)* .... tabungaw
plant- squash, stem .... pamarosan
plant- squash, wax guord *(Benincasa hispida)* .... tangkoy
plant- stick tights, long skinny *(Bidens pilosa)* .... puriket
plant- stick tights, round *(Urena lobata)* .... kullokullot
plant- sugar cane *(Saccharum officinarium)* .... unas
plant- taro *(Colocasia esculenta)* .... aba
plant- taro, shoots of .... daludal
plant- tuber .... bagas
plant- vine for ties *(Donax cannaeformis)* .... daromaka
plant- vine, general term .... lanot
plant- vine, spiny, leguminous *(Caesalpinia crista)* .... dawer
plant- wilt or wither, to .... malaylay
plant- yam *(Dioscorea alata)* .... ubi
plants, flowering .... masetas
plants, to transplant .... agraep

plan, to .... agplano

play, to .... agay-ayam
playing cards .... braha
Please pass the rice. .... Iyawat mo man ti inapuy.
please .... man
plow between rows, to .... agringkon
plow, mound between two lines .... baet
plow, one line .... gulis
plow, to .... agarado
pocket .... bolsa
pockmarked .... burtong
point at, to .... itudo
poison .... lason
poke at an angle .... nasikarod
poke straight, to .... nadalapos
poke through, to .... sumalput
pollen .... nota
poor, not rich .... pubre
possible, can be .... mabalin
pot, cover for .... kalob
pray for dead at cemetery, to .... aglualo
pray, to .... agkararag
precious, dear, highly esteemed .... napateg
prefix indicating similarity .... mara
prepare to leave, to .... agrubbuat, sagana nga pumanaw
prepare, to (food) .... agsagana
prisoner .... balud
probably, very likely .... nalabit
products .... pfabrica
problem, trouble .... problema
profit .... gananshia
promise, to .... ikari, sapata
promise, to break .... matongpal
prompt, fast, quick .... napartak, napaspas, napardas
protect, defend, to .... aganawa
provided that .... no la ketdi
puddle, pool of water .... pilaw
pull up, uproot, to .... agparut
pull, to .... guyod, guyoden
pulverize soil, to .... maburak
punishment .... bawel
pure, purely .... pulos
push, shove, to .... iduron
put away, keep, to .... idulin
put in cage, to .... ikoloong
put, place, to .... ikabil

Q q

QUESTIONS

q.- Certainly, why not? ******* .... Haan, man.
q.- From where (are you?) .... Taga-ano-(ka?)
q.- How are you? (sing) .... Komosta ka?
q.- how long (length)? .... kasano kaattidog?
q.- how long (time)? .... kasano kabayag?
q.- How many days do you stay here? .... Mano nga aldaw nga agnaedka ditoy?
q.- How much for one? .... Sagmamano?
q.- How much, how many? .... Mano?
q.- How old are you? .... Mano ti tawen mo?
q.- How? .... Kasano?
q.- I wonder why? .... Apay ngata?
q.- Is there mail for me? .... Adda kadi surat para kaniak?
q.- May I see please? .... Kitaek, man?
q.- Possible to ask a question? .... Mabalin ti agsaludsud?
q.- What are you doing? .... Ania ti araramidem?
q.- What do you mean? .... Ania ti ipapan mo?
q.- What do you want? .... Ania ti kayat mo?
q.- What happened? .... Ania ti napasamak?
q.- What help can I be to you? .... Ania ti maitulong-ko kenka?
q.- What is the use of it? .... Pangan-anoen na?
q.- What is your name? .... Ania ti nagan mo?
q.- What is your time? .... Ania ti oras mo?
q.- What shall we do? (sing) .... Ania ti aramidta?
q.- What? .... Ania?
q.- When? .... Kaano?
q.- Where are you going? .... Papanam?
q.- Where have you been? .... Nagapuam?
q.- Where? .... Sadino? Ayanna?
q.- Who? .... Sino?
q.- Why not? .... Apay ta saan?
q.- Why? .... Apay?
q.- Why? (expecting a response) .... Apay ngay?
q.- You don't have time? .... Awan oras mo?
q.- You have nothing to do? .... Awan ti aramidem?
q.- You show me please? .... Ipakitam man?

quack doctor .... mangngagas
quarrel, to .... agapa
question marker word .... kadi
question, to .... agsaludsud
quiet, to be (Shut up!) .... Tumalna!

R r

radio .... radyo
rain steady for days, to .... agnepnep
rain, to .... agtudo
rainbow .... bullalayaw
rattan pack .... paseeking
reach, arrive at, to .... danonen
read, to .... agbasa
really, true .... agpayso, telaga (Tag.)
reason, motive .... gapo
reciprocate, return a letter, to .... agsubalitan
refuse, to .... ipaidam
remember, to .... malagip
remembrance, souvenir .... pakalaglagipan
remove charcoal from pit, to .... agadaw
remove rice, corn from ground, to .... agakas
remove, take away, to .... ikkaten, maikkat
rent .... salda, abang
repair, fix, to .... agtarimaan
repeat, reiterate, to .... uliten
resprout, revive, resuscitate, to .... agungar
return, to .... agsubli, isubli

RICE

rice field .... talon
rice- before cooking .... bagas
rice- before removing husk .... irik
rice- cake .... kankanen, (kaan)
rice- cake, round, flat, soft .... bibingka
rice- cold, leftover .... kilabban
rice- cooked .... inapuy
rice- fried .... kinirug
rice- growing .... pagay
rice- nearly cooked, sound of .... agrekrek
rice- paddy, to plow .... agsuyod
rice- server (bowl) .... bandihado
rice- sweet .... diket
rice- to pound .... agbayo
rice- to remove from stem .... agibaut

rich, wealthy .... mayaman, nabaknang
ride, to (animal) .... agsakay
ride, to (car) .... aglugan
rigid, inflexible .... natibker, nasikkil
ring (jewelry) .... singsing

rinse, dishes, to .... agkilnog
ripe .... naloom
ripe, not .... naata
ripe, overripe .... nalusayat
ripen, to .... ipaloom
river .... karayan
road .... kalsada
road, curvey (The road is curvey.) .... Killokillo ti kalsada.
road, rough .... natalteg ti kalsada
roast, to .... ituno
roll up, twist, to .... aglukot, konikonen
roll, to something .... agtulid
rope .... tali
rope break, snap .... napugsat
rope, splice .... sangal
rope, to coil .... agkawikaw
rotten .... nalungtot
rough .... nakersang
round .... nagbukel, nagtimbukel
round & round, to go .... maipulipul
rub, in water (to clean) .... agisisu
rubber .... guma
rubber band .... elastiko
rude, impolite .... nabastos, salawasaw
run, to .... agtaray, tumaray
rust, to .... aglati

S s

sack .... sako
sad .... naliday
safety pin .... aspili
salary .... sueldo
salt .... asin
same time, to do at .... aggiddan, agsabay
sand .... darat
sandpaper .... liha
sap, resin, juice .... tubbug
save, to .... agornong
say, speak, talk, to .... agsao
say, tell, speak, to .... ibaga
says, (he) .... kano, kuna-(na)
scales, fish .... siksik
school .... eskuela
scissors .... kartib
scrape coconut, to .... agigad
scrape feet, to .... karosen
scratch, to .... kudkuden

scrubber, pot .... ugas
sea, ocean .... baybay
search, to .... agsapul, agbirok
seashore .... igid ti baybay
See you again soon. (singular) .... Agkita tan to.
see, recognize, detect, to .... malasin
see, the first time, to .... ipatuldo
seed .... bukel
seed, for sowing .... bini
seed, to broadcast .... agpurruak
seedling .... somelia
seedling, ready for transplanting .... bonobon
seldom, rarely .... sagpaminsan
sell, to .... aglako, ilako

SENSES

sense- hear, to .... agdengngeg, mangngeg
sense- look, see to .... agkita, makita
sense- smell, to .... agangot
sense- taste, to .... raman, ramanan
sense- to feel or perceive .... marikna
sense- touch, to .... agsagid, sagiden

sensitive person .... naarsagid
separate, set apart, to .... ilasin
serve, to .... agserbi
set free, to .... agbulos
sew, to .... agdait
shadow .... aniniwan
shake bottle, to .... agkulog
shake hands, to .... agkamay
shake off, to (like bloodsucker) .... agwarsi
shake, like blanket, to .... agwagsak
shake, to .... aggongon
shallow .... narabaw, ababaw
shape, fit .... tabas
share, to .... iawat
sharpen, to .... agasa
sharpening stone .... pagasaan
She is a beautiful girl. .... Napintas ti balasang.
shell, husk, peel .... ukis
shiny, bright .... nasileng
ship, large boat .... bapor
shoot with rubber band, to .... agpaltik
short, in stature (people) .... pandek

short, insufficient, few .... kurang, manmano
short, low .... ababa
shorten, to .... agpabpababa
shuffle cards .... suk-suk
shy .... mabain
sick, to be .... agsakit, agriggor
side, other .... bangir, ballasiw
sift, to .... agyakayak
sign .... plakard
sign, signature, to .... agparma
silver .... pirak
simpleton, idiot, dolt .... naloko
sin .... basol, babak
sing, to .... agkanta
sink (not float) .... lumned (lenned)
sit close, to .... agsiseksek
sit down, to .... agtugaw
skin peel, to (from sunburn) .... agkulatlat, agkupsit
slap, to .... agsipat
sleeping bag, saddle (for nuang) .... ap-ap
sleeping mat .... ikamen
slice, to .... magalip
slide cart .... patoke
slingshot .... palsiit (lisit)
slip, slide, to .... mauyos, masulnot, malapsut
slippery .... nagalis
slope, hillside .... bakras
slow .... nabuntog
slowly, to go .... agininayad
small, few, very small .... bassit, battit
small, fine .... napinno
smell (stink) .... nabangsit, naangot
smell, bad (food) .... nalangsi, nabangles
smell, good, fragrant .... nabanglo
smoke .... asok
smooth, clean, pure .... nalinis
smooth, soft, sleek .... nalamuyot
snack .... merienda
snack eaten w/ alcoholic drink .... polotan
sneak or ambush, to .... agarodok
so that, in order that .... tapno
soap .... sabon
soft .... nalukneng
soldier .... soldado
someday .... addan ti aldaw
sore, hurt .... nasakit
soup .... digo
soy sauce .... soya
spasm, death .... agkulitadtad

spasm, leg jerk, to .... agkubtar
spasm, to wiggle legs .... agkuyyakuy
spend money, to .... aggastos
spill, to .... mapattog
spit, for roasting .... tudok
splinter .... salugsug
splinter, to get one .... masalugsug
spotted .... labang
spread out, to .... agiwaras
spring (water) .... ubbug
spy, look through a hole .... agsirip, sumirip
squeak, to .... agitit
squeeze (pimple) .... agpigsit
squeeze (to squirt out) .... pumugsit
squid, dried .... pusit
stake, picket .... pasuk
stand on knees, to .... agparintumeng
stand side by side, to .... agabay
stand up, to .... tumakder
stand, butt higher than head .... agpugiit
star .... bituen
star, shooting .... alayap
stare, to .... agperreng, matmatan
startle, to .... makigtot
stay up all night, to .... mapuyat
stay, remain, to .... agbati, ibati
steal, to .... agtakaw
steep, cliff .... derraas
step on, to .... ibaddek
stick to catch chickens .... pabatay
sticky .... napigket
still, silent .... ulimek
stingy .... naimut
stir, to .... agkiwar
stone, rock .... bato
stop briefly in passing, to .... dumagas
stop, stand still, to .... agsardeng, sumardeng
story, tale, to tell a .... agsarita, agistoria
strange phenomenon .... dildillaw
strange weather .... nakadildillaw ti tiempo
string .... galut
striped, streaked .... garit
stroll until no more money, to .... agwayas
stroll, to .... agpasyar
strong, sturdy, vigorous .... napigsa
stubble .... dasdas
study, to .... agadal
stumble, trip, stub toe, to .... maitibkol
Such only is life. .... Kasta laeng ti biag.

suck, to .... agmolmol
sugar .... asukar
sun dry, to .... ibilag
sun, to shine .... aginit
surplus, excess, more than .... surok
swelled, puffed up .... nalimteg (letteg)
swim, to .... aglangoy

T t

take cover, shade, to .... aglinong
take turns, to .... agsublat, sumublat
talk, lots of, babble, chatter .... agtagari
tall, high, lofty .... natayag
tame .... naamo

TASTES

taste- bitter .... napait
taste- sour, tart .... naalsem
taste- strong, tobacco, liquor .... naingel
taste- sweet .... nasam-it
taste- tart, sour, acid, dry .... nasugpet
tasty, appetizing .... nananam

teacher .... maestro
teeth, strip with .... agkilad, apnotan
temper of metal .... tenneb
tender, soft skin, fragile .... narasi
Thank you. .... Agyamanak., Dios ti agngina.
that - near person addressed .... dayta
The choice is yours. .... Sika ti makaammo., Kumpormi kenka.
the same .... parehas, isu met laeng
there - near person addressed .... dita
There is. .... Adda.
There is none. .... Awan.
There is probably none. .... Awan sa.
There probably is. .... Adda sa.
there, far from all .... idiay
therefore .... isunga
they, their .... da
thick, dense, heavy .... napuskol
thin .... naingpis, nakottong
thin or whittle, to .... agkayas
things .... gamit
this - near speaker .... daytoy
thorn, spine, prickle, fishbone .... siit

those (far) .... dagidiay
those (near) .... dagidi
thought .... panunot
thread .... sinulid
throw & hit target .... naishut
throw away, to .... ibelleng
throw, to .... agbarsak
thunder .... gorrood
tie, to .... igalut
tight, taut .... nairut
tilt, to (bottle) .... ipasikig

TIME REFERENCES

time- Sunday .... Domingo
time- Monday .... Lunes
time- Tuesday .... Martes
time- Wednesday .... Mierkoles
time- Thursday .... Huibes
time- Friday .... Viernes
time- Saturday .... Sabado

time- every Sunday .... dinomingo
time- every Monday .... linunes
time- every Tuesday .... minartes
time- every Wednesday .... minerkoles
time- every Thursday .... huinibes
time- every Friday .... tangal viernes
time- every Saturday .... sinabado
time- every day .... inaldaw
time- every other day .... kadda maysa nga aldaw
time- every week .... linnawes
time- every month .... binulan
time- every year .... tinnawen

time- a little while ago .... itattay
time- a long time .... nabayag
time- A week ago Monday .... Idi naminsan nga Lunes.
time- morning, breakfast .... bigat, pangbigat
time- day, lunch .... aldaw, pangaldaw
time- afternoon .... malem
time- evening, night .... rabii
time- always .... kanayon, kankanayon
time- and then .... idi kuan
time- by & by, in a little while .... madamdama
time- early .... nasapa

time- hour .... oras

time- one o'clock .... a la una
time- two o'clock .... a las dos
time- three o'clock .... a las tres
time- four o'clock .... a las kuatro
time- five o'clock .... a las sinko
time- six o'clock .... a las seis
time- seven o'clock .... a las siete
time- eight o'clock .... a las otso
time- nine o'clock .... a las nuebe
time- ten o'clock .... a las djis
time- eleven o'clock .... a las onse
time- twelve o'clock .... a las dose

time- fast, short time .... nalisto
time- formerly .... idi
time- future .... intono
time- I ate a long time ago. .... Nabayag-ak nga nangan.
time- last year .... idi napan (ng)a tawen
time- late .... naladaw
time- late evening .... rumabrabii
time- month, moon .... bulan
time- never .... uray no saan
time- next time .... intono maminsan
time- next year .... intono umay (ng)a tawen
time- now .... itatta
time- once a month .... maminsan iti makabulan
time- once a week .... maminsan iti makadomingo
time- once a year .... maminsan iti makatawen
time- one week .... makadomingo
time- short .... mabiit
time- sometimes .... no dadduma
time- sunrise .... rumrumuar ti init
time- sunset .... lumnek ti init (lennek)
time- this day next week .... lawas
time- three times .... tallo nga daras
time- today .... itatta nga aldaw
time- tomorrow .... intono bigat
time- year .... tawen
time- yesterday .... idi kalman

timid, scared of all .... natakrot
tip or apex .... mordong
tired, to be .... nabannog
to flip up (front of rolling) .... mabattuag
to, for, with me .... kaniak
to, for, with you (sing) .... kenka, kaniam
to, for, with he, she it .... kenkuana, kaniana
to, for, with us (2) .... kadata

to, for, with us (exclusive)........kadakami
to, for, with us (inclusive)........kadatayo
to, for, with you (pl)........kadakayo
to, for, with them........kadakuada, kaniada
tobacco........tabako

TOOLS

tool- ax........wasay
tool- file........garugad
tool- grub hoe........gabion
tool- hammer........martilio
tool- hand saw........ragadi
tool- handle of........putan
tool- hoe, spade, straight handle........sual
tool- nail........lansa
tool- pencil........lapis
tool- plow........arado
tool- plow handle........witiwit
tool- plow shaft........tangbaw
tool- plow tooth........sarapa
tool- plow, digger on........subsub
tool- rake........rik, kalaykay, peruya
tool- tongs........ipit

toothbrush........supilyo
toothpick........ingat
top of, summit........toktok
torn into pieces........pisangen
toss over shoulder, to........apegud
touch, indecently........karawaen
tough, hardy........naandor
town........ili
town, go to........agodong
track, footprint........tugut
trade, to........agsinokat, agkader, agsukat
trail........dalan
train (railroad)........tren
trample, to........ipayat

TREES

tree stump........pungdol
tree- betel nut *(Areca catechu)*........boa
tree- buri palm *(Corypha elata)*........silag
tree- citrus *(Citrus mitis)*........kalamansing

tree- coconut *(Cocos nucifera)* ..... iniug
tree- edible flowers, leguminous *(Sesbania grandiflora)* ..... katuday
tree- fall at roots ..... nabual
tree- fig *(Ficus sp.)* ..... baliti
tree- fruit *(Sandoricum koetjape)* ..... santol
tree- fruit, bread *(Artocarpus cummunis)* ..... pakak
tree- fruits on trunk *(Ficus spp.)* ..... tebbeg
tree- general term ..... kayo
tree- good wood *(Eugenia bordenii)* ..... panglongboyen
tree- hardwood *(Vitex parviflora)* ..... sagat
tree- heartwood ..... bugas
tree- horseradish *(Moringa oleifera)* ..... maronggay
tree- huge leaves *(Semecarpus cuneiformis)* ..... kamiring
tree- java plum *(Eugenia jambolana)* ..... longboy
tree- kapok *(Ceiba pentandra)* ..... kapasanglay
tree- national *(Pterocarpus sp.)* ..... narra
tree- or plant, stem or trunk of ..... poon
tree- palm *(Cordia myxa)* ..... salig
tree- pine ..... saleng
tree- rambutan *(Momordica ovata)* ..... sugud-sugud
tree- sapwood ..... amag
tree- small, leaves like peach *(Cratoxylon blancoi)* ..... baringkokorong
tree- tamarind *(Tamarindus indica)* ..... salamagi
tree- to prune branches ..... masipak
tree- white flowered ..... busbusilak
tree- with edible fruits *(Allaeanthus glaber)* ..... alokon
trees, to cut down ..... agpukan
trees, to cut up ..... agputed

trip, journey ..... biahe
truth ..... pudno
try, attempt, to ..... padasen
turn around ..... tumalikod
turn body ½ way around, to ..... agpusipus
turn on radio, to ..... agpagunyen
turn over, to ..... baliktaden
turn, nut to ..... puligusen
typhoon ..... bagio

U u

ugly, indecent, obscene ..... naalas, na-arti, nalaad
umbrella ..... payong
under, below ..... sirok
understand, to ..... maawatan
until, to ..... aginggana
use, to ..... mausar, usaren

V v

vacation .... bakasion
valley .... oki-oki, longog
vegetables, generic term .... nateng
vein, central, banana leaf .... palatang
very, much .... unay, perme
veterinarian .... vetinario
victorious, to be .... agballigi
view, to .... agbuya
vinegar .... suka
virtuous, blameless, guiltless .... nasingpet
viscous, thick .... napalit
vitamins .... sustancea
voice, deep .... nabangeg
voice, high .... nasinggit
volcano .... bulcan
vote, to .... agbotos

W w

wager at playing cards .... agsugal
wager, bet, to .... agpusta, agtaya
walk, 2 people different roads .... agsinilliwasiw
walk, not able to, lame .... napilay, lupisak, lugpi
walk, to .... magna
wallet .... pitaka
war .... gubat
warm .... katamtaman
wash basin .... palanggana
wash clothes, to .... aglaba
wash dishes, to .... aginnaw
wash face, to .... agdiram-us
wash penis, to .... agkawkaw
wash up, to .... agbuggo
washcloth .... bimpo

WATER

water .... danum
water evaporated, the rice .... matchanan
water plants, to .... agsibug
water system .... nawasa
water well .... gripo, bobon

water- clean, clear .... naliknaw
water- dirty .... nalibeg
water- salty .... naapgad ti danum
water- to fetch .... agsakdo, sumakdo
water- to flow .... agayos
water- to splash .... agsayo
water- to splash with hands .... agsabuag
waves, breakers .... dalluyon

we (exclusive) .... dakami, sikami
we, two (you and I) .... data
weak .... nakapsut, nakapuy
wear by friction, to .... magasgas
wear down teeth, to .... agribrib
wear down, to .... marunot
weather .... tiempo
wedding, marry to .... agkasar, kasar
wedge .... pasingsing, singat, sinsil
weed, generic term .... root
weed, to (garden) .... aglamon
weed- *(Desmodium spp.)* .... taktakup
weed- medicinal *(Blumea balsamifera)* .... subusub
weeds, tall, dense .... nasamek
weight .... sobok
wet .... nabasa
wet (rainy) season .... matutudo
Whatever! .... Uray ania!
wheel .... dalig
wheel run over foot .... nadalison, dumalis
wheeled cart .... rolling, kareton
wheels leave the ground .... ngumato ti dalig
whip, to .... agbaut
whisper, to .... agarasaas
whistle, instrument .... paswit
whistle, to .... agsagawisiw
wick, candle .... mitsa
wick, kerosene lamp .... pabilo
wide .... nabistrad, nalawa
win, to .... mangabak
wind .... angin
wind, sound of .... bumanisbis
winds, hot .... dugudug
wine .... arak
wine- buri palm .... tuba
wine- sugar cane .... basi
winnow, rice .... bigao
winnow, to .... agtaep
wipe off, to .... agpunas

wire .... barut
wire, barbed .... alambre
wonderful, surprising .... nakaskasdaaw
wood plane .... katam
word, term .... sao
work, job .... trabaho, obra
world, the whole .... lubong
worry, to .... agdanag
wrap, to .... agbalkut, agsaput
wrestle, wrist .... agsanggol
wring out, to .... agpespes
wrinkle, to .... agkuritrit, agkerret
write letter, to .... agsurat

Y y

yard .... paraangan
yes .... wen
yes, just so .... wenna
yet, also, more .... pay
you (sing) .... ka, sika
You are welcome. .... Awan ti ania mana.
You ask, please. .... Saludsudem, man.
You come here please. .... Umay-ka, man ditoy.
You help me please. .... Tumulong-ka man.
You hold on good. .... Agkapet-ka nga naimbag.
You look out! .... Lumisi-ka!
You prick! .... Lukdit-mo!
You try your best. .... Padasem ti kabaelam
You wait! .... Aguray-ka!
You'll be the one! .... Sika-on!
yoyo (a toy) .... yoyo

END OF

ENGLISH – ILOKANO DICTIONARY

SECTION 2
ILOKANO – ENGLISH DICTIONARY

ILOKANO – ENGLISH DICTIONARY

(ALPHABETIZED ON ILOKANO)
(ROOT WORDS UNDERLINED)

ILOKANO........**ENGLISH**

A a

a la una .... time- one o'clock
a las djis .... time- ten o'clock
a las dos .... time- two o'clock
a las dose .... time- twelve o'clock
a las kuatro .... time- four o'clock
a las nuebe .... time- nine o'clock
a las onse .... time- eleven o'clock
a las otso .... time- eight o'clock
a las seis .... time- six o'clock
a las siete .... time- seven o'clock
a las sinko .... time- five o'clock
a las tres .... time- three o'clock
aba *(Colocasia esculenta)* .... plant- taro
ababa .... short, low
abaga .... body- shoulder
abagatan .... direction- south
abal-abal .... insect- beetle, june
abbutaw .... hole, for axle
aboos .... insect- ant, red
abukot, barangawid .... nuang cart- harness, back piece
abut .... hole
abuyo .... animal- wild chicken
ad-adu .... more
adayo .... far, distant
Adda kadi surat para kaniak? .... q.- Is there mail for me?
Adda sa. .... There probably is.
Adda ti ibagak kenka. .... I have something to say to you.
Adda ti ipakitak kenka. .... I have something to show you.
Adda. .... There is.
addan ti aldaw .... someday
addang .... body fnc.- footstep, pace
adi .... people- younger brother or sister

adigi .... house post
adu nga daras .... many times
adu .... many

"AG" VERBS

agabay .... stand side by side, to
agabug .... nuang- shake flies off, to
agabuno .... fertilize, to
agadal .... study, to
agadaw .... remove charcoal from pit, to
agakas .... remove rice, corn from ground, to
agakkub .... cover up, to
agal-al .... body fnc.- breathe hard, to
agammol .... body fnc.- suck, baby bottle, etc.
aganak .... body fnc.- be born, to
aganawa .... protect, defend, to
Agang angaw-ak. .... I am joking.
agangot .... sense- smell, to
agani .... harvest rice, to (by hand)
agannad .... careful, cautious, to be
aganos .... patient, to be
agapa .... quarrel, to
agapit, agburas .... harvest, pick fruits, to
agapros .... pet, to
agarab, agpastur, agwayway .... animal- to pasture
agarado .... plow, to
agaramid .... do, make, build, to
agarasaas .... whisper, to
agarbis .... drizzle, to
agarodok .... sneak or ambush, to
agarun, agapuy .... fire, to light
agas .... medicine
agasa .... sharpen, to
agassibay .... arm over shoulder, to put
agatol .... animal- crab
agawawir .... babysit, to
Agawid-ak to. .... I will come home soon.
agawit, agbunag .... carry, to
agay-ayam .... play, to
agayos .... water- to flow
agbado, isuout .... clothes- wear, to
agbaen .... body fnc.- sneeze, to
agbagkat .... lift, to
agbaklay .... carry on shoulder, to
agbalay .... house- to build a
agbalkut, agsaput .... wrap, to
agballigi .... victorious, to be

agbalsig, balsigen ... chop, to
agbantay ... guard, watch, to
agbarsak ... throw, to
agbasa ... read, to
agbatangtang ... gong, to
agbati, ibati ... stay, remain, to
agbaut ... whip, to
agbayad ... pay, to
agbayo ... rice- to pound
agbekkel ... hang by neck, to
agberber ... expose oneself to the wind, to
agbiag, mabiag ... live (alive)
agbitin ... hang, to (on back of jeepney)
agbotos ... vote, to
agbuggo ... wash up, to
agbugsut ... dying, death struggle
agbulos ... set free, to
agburis ... body fnc.- diarrhea, to have
agbusina ... blow horn, to
agbuya ... view, to
agdait ... sew, to
agdallapeg ... body fnc.- tap fingers, to
agdan ... ladder
agdanag ... worry, to
agdaras, darasen ... hurry, to
agdaringongo ... body fnc.- nosebleed, to
agdata ... lie on back, to
agdengngeg, mangngeg ... sense- hear, to
agdigos ... bathe, to
agdilpat, dilapen ... lick, to
agdiram-us ... wash face, to
agdisso ... bird- alight, to
agdumug ... incline or bend the head, to
aggabor, magaboran ... dirt, to cover with
aggadgad ... corn, to shell w/ nail & board
aggango ... dry, to
aggapas ... harvest rice, to
aggapo ... from (place)
aggaradugud ... body fnc.- stomach growl, to
aggastos ... spend money, to
aggiddan, agsabay ... same time, to do at
aggidigid ... nuang rub against tree, etc.
aggongon ... shake, to
aghardin ... garden, to
agibaut ... rice- to remove from stem
agibuson ... mail, to
agidda ... lie down, to
agigaaw ... dry season
agigad ... scrape coconut, to

agiggam .... hold, to
agimun .... jealous, for wife
Aginagaw ti sipnget ken lawag. .... Changes light to night (dusk).
aginana .... body fnc.- short rest, to take a
aginat .... body fnc.- stretch, to-upon waking
aginggana .... until, to
agininayad .... slowly, to go
aginit .... sun, to shine
aginnaw .... wash dishes, to
aginson .... burn, pile & burn brush
Aginturturog-na .... body fnc.- sleep, to pretend, He is
agirig .... lean, to
agisem .... body fnc.- smile, to
agisisu .... rub, in water (to clean)
agitit .... squeak, to
agiwaras .... spread out, to
agkablaaw, kumablaaw .... greet, welcome, to
agkadua, kumuyog .... accompany, to
agkakok .... knock, to
agkalawikiw .... animal- dog, to wag tail
agkamada .... pile, to make
agkamat .... chase, to
agkamay .... shake hands, to
agkamet .... eat with hands, to
agkammel, agkalap .... fish with hands, to
agkanaldook .... body fnc.- swallow, sound of
agkanta .... sing, to
Agkapet-ka nga naimbag. .... You hold on good.
agkapon .... animal- testicles, to remove
agkararag .... pray, to
agkaras .... bail out, to
agkaryada .... carry cargo for somebody, to
agkasar, kasar .... wedding, marry to
agkatawa .... body fnc.- laugh, to
agkawikaw .... rope, to coil
agkawkaw .... wash penis, to
agkayas .... thin or whittle, to
agkidel .... pinch, to
agkidem .... body fnc.- eyes, to close
agkilad, apnotan .... teeth, strip with
agkilnog .... rinse, dishes, to
agkinod .... body- penis, to move in erection
agkirem .... body fnc.- blink eyes, to
agkiskis .... body fnc.- shave, to
Agkita tan to. .... See you again soon. (singular)
agkita, makita .... sense- look, see to
agkiwar .... stir, to
agkogit .... body- circumcise, to
agkordon .... clothes- shoes, to lace

agkotak .... animal- chicken, cackle
agkubtar .... spasm, leg jerk, to
agkuenta .... account, compute, to
agkulatlat, agkupsit .... skin peel, to (from sunburn)
agkulitadtad .... spasm, death
agkulog .... shake bottle, to
agkuritrit, agkerret .... wrinkle, to
agkutengteng .... guitar, sound of
agkuti .... move, stir, to
agkutikut .... clean with fingers (ear, nose)
agkuyyakuy .... spasm, to wiggle legs
aglaba .... wash clothes, to
aglaban, agdanog .... fight, to
aglako, ilako .... sell, to
aglambong .... boil vegetables or meat, to
aglamon .... weed, to (garden)
aglangoy .... swim, to
aglapitog .... blister, burn, to (sunburn)
aglastog, bulataw .... lie, fib, to
aglati .... rust, to
aglayos .... flood, to
aglemmeng, sumoksok, aglinged .... hide or conceal, to
aglibas .... leave secretly, escape, to
agling-et .... body fnc.- sweat, to
aglinong .... take cover, shade, to
agliwliw .... fish with rod, to
aglualo .... pray for dead at cemetery, to
aglugan .... ride, to (car)
aglukot, konikonen .... roll up, twist, to
agluto .... cook, to
agmama .... chew betel nut, to
agmaya .... animal- nuang mate, to
agmaymaysa .... alone, solitary, to be
agmolmol .... suck, to
agmula, imula .... plant, to
agmulumog .... body fnc.- gargle, to
agnepnep .... rain steady for days, to
agngalngal, karat-om .... body fnc.- chew, to
agngatingat .... animal- chew cud, to
agnginaw .... body fnc.- conceive child, to
agngoak .... nuang- voice of
agobo .... leak, to
agodong .... town, go to
agoklap .... banana- flower, to open
agokrad .... open, to (flower)
agong .... body- nose
agornong .... save, to
agorok .... body fnc.- snore, to
agottog .... body fnc.- horny, to be

agpabpababa	shorten, to
agpagunyen	turn on radio, to
agpakleb (kelleb)	lie on stomach, to
agpalad	palms, to read
agpalakpak	applaud, to
agpalennek	kill time, to
agpalpa	food settle (in stomach), to
agpaltik	shoot with rubber band, to
agpanateng	body fnc.- cold, to have a
agpangres	body fnc.- blow nose, to
agparintumeng	stand on knees, to
agparma	sign, signature, to
agparti	butcher, to
agparut	pull up, uproot, to
agpasyar	stroll, to
agpatakder	construct, to (house, building)
agpatodon	blame, to shift
agpayapay	nuang- wiggle ears, to
agpayat	pack (dirt), to
agpayso, telaga (Tag.)	really, true
agperreng, matmatan	stare, to
agpespes	wring out, to
agpessa	animal- hatch, egg
agpidut	pick up, to
agpigsit	squeeze (pimple)
agpintar	paint, to
agplano	plan, to
agpolting	harvest by cutting stem, to
agpugiit	stand, butt higher than head
agpukan	trees, to cut down
agpukis	body fnc.- haircut, to have
agpukkaw, ayaban	holler or call, to
agpunas	wipe off, to
agpuor, mapuor	burn, scorch, forest fire, to
agpurruak	seed, to broadcast
agpurus	harvest anything, to
agpusi, mapusi	corn, to shell
agpusipus	turn body ½ way around, to
agpusta, agtaya	wager, bet, to
agputed	trees, to cut up
agpuyot	blow on, to
agraep	plants, to transplant
Agragsak-tayo.	Let's rejoice. (pl)
agrakrak	destroy or ruin, to
agrekrek	rice- nearly cooked, sound of
agribrib	wear down teeth, to
agriing	body fnc.- awake, to
agrikrikos, agliklikaw	go around in circles, to
agringkon	plow between rows, to

agrittok ... body fnc.- crack knuckles, to
agrubbuat, sagana nga pumanaw ... prepare to leave, to
agrungrung ... cigarette, to put out
agsabet, sumabet ... meet, to
agsabuag ... water- to splash with hands
agsagad ... harrow, to
agsagana ... prepare, to (food)
agsagawisiw ... whistle, to
agsagid, sagiden ... sense- touch, to
agsaiddek ... body fnc.- hiccough, to
agsakasaka ... barefoot, to go
agsakay ... ride, to (animal)
agsakdo, sumakdo ... water- to fetch
agsakit, agriggor ... sick, to be
agsala ... dance, to
agsalensen ... pile, make a big (overburden)
agsalingsing ... clean, bamboo knuckles, to
agsalsal, isalsal ... body fnc.- masturbate, to
agsaludsud ... question, to
agsangdo ... nuangs to fight, butt heads
agsanggol ... wrestle, wrist
agsangit, aglua ... body fnc.- weep, cry, to
agsanud, tres ... backwards, to go
agsao ... say, speak, talk, to
agsaplit ... nuang- wag tail
agsapul, agbirok ... search, to
agsardeng, sumardeng ... stop, stand still, to
agsarita, agistoria ... story, tale, to tell a
agsarua ... body fnc.- vomit, to
agsasalisal ... compete, contest, to
agsaur ... cheat, to
agsayo ... water- to splash
agsedsed, agdidikket ... closer, move to
agseg-am ... body fnc.- clear throat, to
agsendi ... cigarette, to light from another
agserbi ... serve, to
agsibug ... water plants, to
agsiddaaw ... amaze, to be
agsikig ... lie on side, to
agsilud ... insect- sting, to (bee sting)
agsinabali ... disagree, to
agsinga ... light a lamp, to
agsingat ... fill, a crack, to
agsingir ... collect debt, to
agsinglag ... extract oil, to
agsinglut ... body fnc.- sniff, to
agsinilliwasiw ... walk, 2 people different roads
agsinit ... burn yourself, to
agsinokat, agkader, agsukat ... trade, to

agsipat … slap, to
agsippaw … catch something thrown, to
agsipsip … grass- to trim
agsirip, sumirip … spy, look through a hole
agsiseksek … sit close, to
agsisir … fray, to
agsosoon … carry on head, to
agsubalitan … reciprocate, return a letter, to
agsublat, sumublat … take turns, to
agsubli, isubli … return, to
agsubsub … animal- pig digging or rooting
agsugal … wager at playing cards
agsurat … write letter, to
agsuro, isuro … learn, to
agsuyaab … body fnc.- yawn, to
agsuyod … rice- paddy, to plow
agtabas, agsiprau … grass- to cut
agtaep … winnow, to
agtagainep … body fnc.- dream, to
agtagari … talk, lots of, babble, chatter
agtakaw … steal, to
agtaktak … delay, detain, to
agtaliaw, tumaliaw … look behind, backwards, to
agtan-aw, tuman-aw … look down, to
agtapaya … hold at arms length, to
agtaraken … animals- to raise
agtaraok … animal- rooster, to crow
agtaray, tumaray … run, to
agtarimaan … repair, fix, to
agtarindanum … body- athletes foot, to have
agtaul … animal- dog, to bark
agtayab … bird- fly, to
agtebba … harvest bananas, to
agtedted … drip, trickle, leak, to
agtestes … chain saw, to use
agtig-ab … body fnc.- burp, to
agtigariger … body fnc.- shiver, to
agtiliw … catch, to (like a chicken)
agtimbeng … balance, to
agtinnulong … help each other, to
agtiritir … flip over, to
agtonged … nuang- to stimulate milk supply
agtopra … body fnc.- spit, to
agtubo … grow, to
agtudo … rain, to
agtugaw … sit down, to
agtulid … roll, to something
agtungrow … banana- sick plantation
agud-ud, tumawar … haggle or bargain, to

agukis, buksilan .... husk, to
agungar .... resprout, revive, resuscitate, to
agungik .... animal- pig, to oink
Aguray-ka! .... You wait!
agusus .... eat sugar cane, to
aguyek .... body fnc.- cough, to
agwagsak .... shake, like blanket, to
agwagwag .... clean, grass, etc, to
agwaliwali .... body- teeth to be loose
agwarsi .... shake off, to (like bloodsucker)
agwayas .... stroll until no more money, to
agyakayak .... sift, to
Agyamanak., Dios ti agngina. .... Thank you.
agyan .... dwell, to
agyut .... body- sexual intercourse, to have

END "AG" VERBS

ak, siak .... I, me
akikid .... narrow
aklo .... house- ladle
akut-akut .... insect- wasp, mud
al-alia .... ghost
alad .... fence, hedge
alaen .... get, to
alambre .... wire, barbed
alayap .... star, shooting
aldaw, pangaldaw .... time- day, lunch
alibut .... animal- lizard, brown
alibuyong .... overcast
alig .... insect- bee, small
alimatek, alinta .... animal- leech
alimbubuyog .... insect- wasp, bumblebee
alingo .... animal- wild pig
alipuspus .... body- hair, whorl in the
alladan .... grass- the sharp kind
alokon *(Allaeanthus glaber)* .... tree- with edible fruits
alumbuyod .... animal- worm
alumpipinig .... insect- wasp
alupasi .... banana- dry sheath of leaf
alutiit .... animal- lizard, house
amag .... tree- sapwood
amianan .... direction- north
amin .... all, total
ammo .... know, to
amor, linnaaw .... dew
anak .... people- child
anay .... insect- termite

anchokos .... eye glasses
angin .... wind
anglit .... body odor
anguyob .... blow pipe
Ania ti aramidta? .... q.- What shall we do? (sing)
Ania ti araramidem? .... q.- What are you doing?
Ania ti ipapan mo? .... q.- What do you mean?
Ania ti kayat mo? .... q.- What do you want?
Ania ti maitulong-ko kenka? .... q.- What help can I be to you?
Ania ti nagan mo? .... q.- What is your name?
Ania ti napasamak? .... q.- What happened?
Ania ti oras mo? .... q.- What is your time?
Ania? .... q.- What?
animales .... animal- general term
aniniwan .... shadow
antutungal .... insect- ant, black
ap-ap .... sleeping bag, saddle (for nuang)
apalido .... name, family
Apay ngata? .... q.- I wonder why?
Apay ta saan? .... q.- Why not?
Apay ngay? .... q.- Why? (expecting a response)
Apay? .... q.- Why?
apegud .... toss over shoulder, to
aplat .... insect- aphid
apo .... people- grandparent
apuy .... fire
arado .... tool- plow
arak .... wine
ararawan .... insect- mole cricket
asawa .... people- wife, husband, mate
asideg .... near
asin .... salt
aso .... animal- dog
asok .... smoke
aspili .... safety pin
asukar .... sugar
atep .... house- roof
atiddog .... long
atis *(Arnona squamosa)* .... fruit- sweetsop
Awan oras ko. .... I have no time.
Awan problema. .... No problem.
Awan sa. .... There is probably none.
Awan ti ania mana. .... You are welcome.
Awan ti aramidek. .... I have nothing to do.
Awan ti aramidem? .... q.- You have nothing to do?
Awan ti biang mo. .... None of your business.
Awan ti oras mo? .... q.- You don't have time?
Awan uray maysa. .... Not even one.
Awan. .... There is none.

awanan .... house- wall header
awisen .... persuade to come
Ayayat-enka. .... I love you. (sing)
ayukan .... insect- wasp, yellow jacket
azul .... color- blue

B b

baag .... g-string
babai .... people- woman, female
babain *(Mimosa pudica)* .... plant- sensitive
babawi .... indian giver
baboy .... animal- pig, hog
bado .... clothes
baet .... plow, mound between two lines
bagas .... plant- tuber
bagas .... rice- before cooking
bagi .... body
bagio .... typhoon
bagis .... body- intestine, guts
bagoten .... lift kamote vine, to
bagtit .... crazy
baka .... animal- cow, cattle
baka-baka .... insect- beetle, red & black
bakano .... like that
bakasion .... vacation
baket .... people- woman, old
bakir .... forest
bakla .... people- homosexual
bakrang .... body- side of the
bakras .... slope, hillside
bala .... bullet
balasang .... people- woman, single, unmarried
balatong *(Phaseolus radiatus)* .... plant- bean, mungo
balay .... house
balikid .... back of something, reverse
baliktaden .... turn over, to
baliti *(Ficus sp.)* .... tree- fig
balitok .... gold
balkon .... house- porch, balcony
balud .... prisoner
balun .... lunch, provisions
banay .... plant- 6' tall, big long leaves
banban .... bamboo ties
banda (Ania ti banda?) .... direction- (What direction?)
bandera .... flag
bandihado .... rice- server (bowl)
bangad .... buneng, back of

bangbangsit *(Hyptis suaveolens)*........ plant- smelly
bangir, ballasiw........ side, other
bangkag........ farm, upland
bangking........ leaning, unequal
banias........ animal- iguana
banka........ boat, small
bantay........ mountain
baonen........ errand, to go on
bapor........ ship, large boat
baranggay........ municipality, part of
barbareng, sapay la koma........ hope
barbas........ body- beard
baridbid........ clothes- headband
baringkokorong *(Cratoxylon blancoi)*........ tree- small leaves like peach tree
barong........ people- groom
barrairong........ insect- coconut beetle
bartin........ animal- snake, green
baru........ people- bachelor, new
barukong........ body- chest
barut........ wire
barya........ money- coins
basi........ wine- sugar cane
baso........ house- glass, drinking
basol, babak........ sin
bassit, battit........ small, few, very small
basta, huston........ enough, stop
bateria........ battery
batikola........ nuang cart- harness
bato........ stone, rock
bawang *(Allium sativum)*........ plant- garlic
bawel........ punishment
bayabas........ fruit- guava
bayangbayang........ house- gable end of
bayaw........ people- brother-in-law
baybay........ sea, ocean
bayug, bikal, bolo, kawayan........ bamboo- varieties
bayyek........ animal- tadpole
bennek........ animal- clam
berde........ color- green
biahe........ trip, journey
biang........ care, concern
bibig........ body- lips
bibingka........ rice- cake, round, flat, soft
bigao........ winnow, rice
bigat, pangbigat........ time- morning, breakfast
bilangen........ count, to
bilid........ fruits- ridges on
billit........ bird
bimpo........ washcloth

bingkol .... dirt, clump of
bini .... seed, for sowing
binting .... money- 25 cent piece
binulan .... time- every month
biroroko .... animal- snail, big, land
birri .... crack, small, in board
bisikleta .... bicycle
bisita .... people- visitor
bisukol .... animal- snail, edible
bituen .... star
boa *(Areca catechu)* .... tree- betel nut
bobongan .... house- peak of
boggoong .... fish sauce
bokayo .... candy, coconut balls
boko .... body- knuckle (or bamboo knuckle)
bola .... ball
bolsa .... pocket
bonobon .... seedling, ready for transplanting
bo-ok .... body- hair, of the head
boot .... mold
botelia .... bottle
botonis .... button
braha .... playing cards
buaya .... animal- crocodile
budo .... insect- itchy hairs of caterpillar
budwa-budwan .... insect- caterpillar
bugas .... tree- heartwood
bugi .... body- leg, calf of
buk-buk .... insect- beetle, rice
bukarelyo .... candy, flat coconut
bukel .... seed
bukot, likod .... body- back
buksit, tian .... body- stomach
bulag .... body- blind
bulan .... time- month, moon
bulcan .... volcano
bulding .... body- one-eyed
bulig .... banana bundle
bullalayaw .... rainbow
bulog .... animal- bull
bulong .... leaf, (plant, book, etc.)
bumaba, umulog, sumalog .... descend, to
bumangon .... body fnc.- rise, to get up
bumanisbis .... wind, sound of
bumbilia .... bulb, flashlight, etc.
bumtak (bettak) .... explode, to
bumulod .... borrow, to
buneng .... bolo, machete
bunga .... fruit

bungal .... corn, few kernels on cob
bungbung .... bamboo bomb
buniag .... baptism
burias .... animal- piglet
burik .... color- able to change
burtong .... pockmarked
busbusilak .... tree- white flowered
busel .... fruit- small
buta .... clothes- boots
butbut .... clothes- hole in
buto .... body- penis

D d

da .... they, their
daan .... old, stale
daga .... dirt, soil, earth
dagidi .... those (near)
dagidiay .... those (far)
dagum .... needle
dagus .... immediately
dakami, sikami .... we (exclusive)
dakes .... bad, evil
dakkel .... large, big
dakulap .... body- palm of hand
dalag .... animal- mudfish
dalan .... trail
dalayday .... nuang- cart for cant
daldaligan *(Averrhoa carambola)* .... fruit- starfruit
dalem .... body- liver
dalig .... wheel
dalikan .... house- hearth, stove
dalluyon .... waves, breakers
daludal .... plant- taro, shoots of
damag .... news
damortis *(Pithecolobium dulce)* .... plant- bean, tree
dandani, nganngani, nagistayan .... nearly, almost
dangaw .... insect- stink bug
danonen .... reach, arrive at, to
danum .... water
dapan .... body- foot, sole of
dapo .... ashes, grey
dara .... body- blood
darat .... sand
daromaka *(Donax cannaeformis)* .... plant- vine for ties
dasdas .... stubble
data .... we, two (you and I)
datar .... house- floor

dati, gagangay, latta, sigud .... from before
dawer *(Caesalpinia crista)* .... plant- vine, spiny, leguminous
daya .... direction- east
dayawen .... honor, to
dayta .... that - near person addressed
daytoy .... this - near speaker
delikado .... fragile, dangerous
derraas .... steep, cliff
destinio .... destination
diablo .... devil
Diak ammo., Madik ammo. .... I don't know.
Diak kayat., Haan ko nga kayat. .... I don't want (like).
Diak malagip., Madik malagip. .... I don't remember.
diding .... house- wall
digo .... soup
diken-diken .... insect- millipede
diket .... rice- sweet
dila .... body- tongue
dildillaw .... strange phenomenon
dinardaraan .... meat, cooked in blood
dingoen .... animals, back yard
dinomingo .... time- every Sunday
Dios .... God
dipperentia .... difference
dippig, lakatan, kanton, guyod .... banana- varieties
diretso .... direction- straight ahead
diro .... honey
dita .... there - near person addressed
ditoy .... here - near speaker
Domingo .... time- Sunday
dori-dori .... body- back bone
dua pulo, biente (Sp.) .... number- twenty
dua, dos (Sp.) .... number- two
dudon .... insect- grasshopper
dugudug .... winds, hot
dugul .... bump, a
dumagas .... stop briefly in passing, to
dumawat .... beg, ask, to
dutdut .... animal- chicken feathers or hair
dutdut .... body- hair, feathers
duyaw .... color- yellow

E e

ehe .... axle
elastiko .... rubber band
eleksion .... election
en .... already

eppes ... empty, ears of grain, seeds
eskuela ... school
espeltado ... highway

G g

gabion ... tool- grub hoe
gaddil ... banana- spots on
gagabuten *(Eleusine indica)* ... grass- yard
galunggung ... fish, small dried
galut ... string
gamit ... things
gananshia ... profit
gansa ... gong
gapo ... reason, motive
garapon ... jar
garit ... striped, streaked
garugad ... tool- file
gata, getta ... milk, coconut
gatas ... milk
gawat ... famine, time of scarcity
gawed *(Ehretia navesii)* ... plant- betel pepper
gayaman ... insect- centipede
gayyem ... people- friend
getget ... nuang- notches on yoke
gettang ... crack, in glass
gikgik ... bird- white breast, black beak
gingined ... earthquake
giwang ... chicken, crack in tail, breach
gloria, dato, tumok, seniorita ... banana- varieties
gorabis ... matches
gorong ... body- ankle
gorrood ... thunder
grabi ... many many
gripo, bobon ... water well
guantis ... clothes- gloves
gubat ... war
gulis ... plow, one line
guma ... rubber
gumatang ... buy, purchase, to
gunnot ... fruit- flesh of
gusing ... knife- small nick in blade
guyod, guyoden ... pull, to

H h

Haan nga bale! .... Never mind!
Haan, man. .... q.- Certainly, why not? *******
hegante .... giant
Huibes .... time- Thursday
huinibes .... time- every Thursday
hulin .... marble
husto .... correct, right

I i

iawat .... share, to
iawid .... home, to take home
Iawid-ko dayta. .... I will take that home.
ibaddek .... step on, to
ibaga .... say, tell, speak, to
ibelleng .... throw away, to
ibilag .... sun dry, to
iddepen .... extinguish, to
idi kalman .... time- yesterday
idi kuan .... time- and then
Idi naminsan nga Lunes. .... time- A week ago Monday.
idi napan (ng)a tawen .... time- last year
idi .... time- formerly
idiay .... there, far from all
idulin .... put away, keep, to
iduron .... push, shove, to
igalut .... tie, to
igawgaw .... clothes- to rinse
igges .... insect- worms in fruits
igid ti baybay .... seashore
igid .... edge, margin
iit .... leaf, central vein
ikabil .... put, place, to
ikali, agkali .... dig a hole, to
ikamen .... sleeping mat
ikandado, makatolbek .... lock the door, to
ikari, sapata .... promise, to
ikelso .... chock wheel, to
ikkaten, maikkat .... remove, take away, to
ikoloong .... put in cage, to
ilasin .... separate, set apart, to
ili .... town
ilingta .... boil, eggs, to
ima .... body- hand
imbitar .... invitation
imbudo .... funnel

imburnal .... culvert
importante .... important
imptog .... body- erection
inaldaw .... time- every day
inapuy .... rice- cooked
ingat .... toothpick
iniug *(Cocos nucifera)* .... tree- coconut
innem, seis (Sp.) .... number- six
insekto .... insect- general term
insik .... people- Chinese person
intono bigat .... time- tomorrow
intono umay (ng)a tawen .... time- next year
intono .... time- future
intono maminsan .... time- next time
ipabulod .... lend, to
ipaidam .... refuse, to
Ipakitam man? .... q.- You show me please?
ipaloom .... ripen, to
ipalpal .... nails, to drive
ipalubos .... allow, to
ipasikig .... tilt, to (bottle)
ipattog .... empty, to
ipatuldo .... see, the first time, to
ipawit .... carry to somebody, to
ipayat .... trample, to
ipes .... insect- cockroach
ipit .... tool- tongs
iprito .... fry, to
ipus .... animal- tail
irik .... rice- before removing husk
irikep .... close door, window
irugi .... begin, commence, to
isawsaw .... dip (like bread in coffee)
isilpo .... join two items, lengthen
isu, isuna .... he, she, it
isunga .... therefore
itatta nga aldaw .... time- today
itatta .... time- now
itattay .... time- a little while ago
ited .... give, to
itik .... animal- duck, brown
itlog .... egg
itudo .... point at, to
itugot .... bring, to
ituno .... roast, to
iyakar .... nuang- to move
Iyawat mo man ti inapuy. .... Please pass the rice.

K k

ka, sika .... you (sing)
Kaano? .... q.- When?
kaapapan-(na) .... just left (he)
kaaroba .... people- neighbor
kabagian .... people- relatives
kaban .... measure- 75 liters
kabassiten .... most- smallest
kabatiti *(Luffa cylindrica)* .... fruit- like a cucumber
kabayo .... animal- horse
kabosor, kasuron, kagurra .... enemy
kabsat .... people- brother, sister
kabus .... moon, full
kadakami .... to, for, with us (exclusive)
kadakayo .... to, for, with you (pl)
kadakuada, kaniada .... to, for, with them
kadata .... to, for, with us (2)
kadatayo .... to, for, with us (inclusive)
kadakkelen .... most- biggest
kadda maysa nga aldaw .... time- every other day
kadi .... question marker word
kadikketen nga gayyem .... most- best friend
kadkadua .... body- afterbirth
kadua .... people- companion
kaguddua .... measure- one-half (1/2)
kaha, kahon .... box, case
kaingingas .... body- face, similar
kaka .... people- elder brother or sister
kakaasi .... pitiful, woeful
kakapat .... measure- one-fourth (1/4)
kalakyan .... nuang calf- male
kalamansing *(Citrus mitis)* .... tree- citrus
kalapati .... bird- pigeon
kalapaw .... hut, rest
kalbo .... body- hair, no
kalburo .... carbide
kaldero .... kettle
kalding .... animal- goat
kalenderio .... calendar
kallogong .... clothes- hat
kalob .... pot, cover for
kalombida .... nuang- short rope for yoke
kalsada .... road
kaluban .... buneng, sheath for
kamanaw .... body- skin, white spots on
kamarines, baguio, tondal .... banana- varieties
kamatis .... fruit- tomato
kamiring *(Semecarpus cuneiformis)* .... tree- huge leaves

kamoras .... measles
kamoro .... body- pimple
kamsut .... cant hook
kanawan .... direction- right
kanayon, kankanayon .... time- always
kandela .... candle
kaniak .... to, for, with me
kanigid .... direction- left
kankanen, (kaan) .... rice- cake
kano, kuna-(na) .... says, (he)
Kapangpangan-ko. .... I just ate.
kapas .... cotton
kapasanglay *(Ceiba pentandra)* .... tree- kapok
kapateria .... coffee maker, teapot
kaper .... body- smegma
kapi .... coffee
kapintasen .... most- most beautiful
kapon .... animal- castrated
kapote .... clothes- rain coat
kapuyo .... body- blister
karabasa .... plant- squash
karabukob .... body- throat
karawaen .... touch, indecently
karayan .... river
karaykayen .... animal- chicken scratching
kardis *(Cajanus cajan)* .... plant- pea, pigeon
karegaten .... most- most difficult
karma .... body- soul
karne .... meat
karnero .... animal- sheep
karosen .... scrape feet, to
karot .... fruit- carrot
kartib .... scissors
kas .... as, like
kasabaan .... banana plantation
Kasano kaattidog? .... q.- How long (length)?
Kasano kabayag? .... q.- How long (time)?
Kasano? .... q.- How?
kasdiay .... like that
kasig .... nuang cart- box on
kasilias .... house- bathroom
kasinsin .... people- cousin
Kasta laeng ti biag. .... Such only is life.
kasta .... like that
kastoy .... like this
katam .... wood plane
katamtaman .... warm
katangkenen .... most- hardest
kategan .... boundary

katre .... house- bed
katuday *(Sesbania grandiflora)* .... tree- edible flowers, leguminous
kawar .... chain
kawit .... hook
kawitan .... animal- rooster
Kayat ko. .... I like, want.
kaykay .... broom, outdoor
kayo .... tree- general term
keggang .... body- scab
ken, ket .... and
kenka, kaniam .... to, for, with you (sing)
kenkuana, kaniana .... to, for, with he, she it
kiaw .... bird- oriole
kibol, putot .... animal- tail, no
kibong-kibong .... body- vulva
kiday-kiday .... body- eyebrow
kilabban .... rice- cold, leftover
kilawen .... eat raw, to
kili-kili .... body- armpit
kiling .... bamboo- varieties
Killokillo ti kalsada. .... road, curvey (The road is curvey.)
kimat .... lightning
kinirug .... rice- fried
kinni-kinni .... animal- duck waddle
kissit .... body- sperm
Kitaek, man? .... q.- May I see please?
kittool .... insect- beetle, click
klasse .... kind, type, species
koko .... body- fingernail
Komosta ka ? .... q.- How are you? (sing)
kongkong, mangabuyo .... bird- small, hawklike
kopinen .... fold cloth, to
korkoridong .... bird- nuang
kosina .... house- kitchen
koto .... insect- head louse
koton .... insect- ant, general name
kotse .... automobile, car
kua .... general term for anything
kuantong *(Mmaranthus viridis)* .... plant- amaranth
kuarta .... money
kuarto .... house- room
kudil .... body- skin
kudkuden .... scratch, to
kuentas .... necklace, rosary
kuesa .... cheese
Kukuada. .... own- They own.
Kukuak. .... own- I own.
Kukuakayo. .... own- You (pl) own.
Kukuam. .... own- You own. (sing)

Kukuami. .... own- We (exclusive) own.
Kukuana. .... own- He, She, It owns.
Kukuata. .... own- We (2) own.
Kukuatayo. .... own- We (inclusive) own.
kulalanti .... insect- firefly
kulba .... nuang cart- wood for axle
kulibangbang .... insect- butterfly
kulipato .... bird- night hawk
kullokullot *(Urena lobata)* .... plant- stick tights, round
kulot .... body- hair, curly
kumagat .... insect- bite, to mosquitoes, etc.
kumotkottong .... body- getting thinner
kumpay .... knife- rice
kumpit, kutsilio .... knife
kumugtar .... kick, to
kundidit .... insect- cicada
kurang, manmano .... short, insufficient, few
kurarapnit .... animal- bat, small
kurente .... electricity, current
kuriat .... insect- cricket
kuriit .... body- anus
kurimatmat .... body- eyelash
kutsara .... house- spoon

L l

labang .... spotted
labba .... house- basket with handles
labintador .... firecracker
laeng .... only
lakasa .... house- foot locker
lakay .... people- man, old
lalaki .... people- man, male
lalat, callio .... body- callus
lambi-lambi .... animal- chicken wattles
lames .... animal- fish, fresh water
lamisaan .... house- table
lamok .... insect- mosquito
lamolamo, silalabus .... body- naked
lana .... oil, coconut
landok .... iron
langdet .... chopping block
langit .... heaven, sky, paradise
langka *(Artocarpus integrifolia)* .... fruit- jack
lanot .... plant- vine, general term
lansa .... tool- nail
lansita .... knife- pocket
lapayag .... body- ears

lapis .... tool- pencil
lasag .... body- flesh
lasi .... body- dandruff
lason .... poison
lasona *(Allium cepa)* .... plant- onion
lata .... can, tin
lateg .... body- penis, shaft of
laud .... direction- west
lawas .... time- this day next week
lawwa-lawwa .... insect- spider
laya *(Zingiber officinale)* .... plant- ginger
letra .... letter, alphabetic character
letrato .... photo
libre .... free, no charge
libro .... book
lidda *(Saccharum spontaneum)* .... grass- coarse, tall
liha .... sandpaper
likkalikkaong .... broken or rolling ground
likkaong .... holes in road, field, etc
lima, sinko (Sp.) .... number- five
linnawes .... time- every week
linnid .... moon, new
linteg .... law, rule
linunes .... time- every Monday
lip-ak .... peel, leaves, like onion
lipay-lipay .... body- ankle bone
littoko *(Calamus sp.)* .... fruit- rattan
longboy *(Eugenia jambolana)* .... tree- java plum
longon .... coffin
lua .... body- tears
lubnak .... nuang wallow
lubong .... world, the whole
lugar .... place, spot
lugit .... bird manure
lukatan .... open
lukban *(Citrus decumana)* .... fruit- pomelo
Lukdit-mo! .... You prick!
Lumabas-ak laeng. .... I am only passing.
lumagto .... jump, to
Lumisi-ka! .... You look out!
lumned (lenned) .... sink (not float)
lumnek ti init (lennek) .... time- sunset
lumot .... moss
lumpaso .... coconut husk floor polisher
lumuklukmeg .... body- getting fatter
lumumba .... overtake & pass
Lunes .... time- Monday
lupot .... cloth, rag
luppo .... body- thigh

lupus .... animal- snake skin (shed)

M m

maabak............ lose, to, or be defeated
maabungan .... body- skin, covered
maawatan............ understand, to
mabain .... shy
Mabalin nga ma-angot-nak?............ body- Can you smell me?
Mabalin ti agsaludsud? .... q.- Possible to ask a question?
mabalin .... possible, can be
mabattuag .... to flip up (front of rolling)
mabiit............ time- short
Mabisin-ak. .... I am hungry.
mabistak............ crack in board
maburak............ pulverize soil, to
maburek, ipaburek............ boil, to
mabuteng, agbuteng .... afraid, to be
madamdama .... time- by & by, in a little while
Madi ti riknak. .... I feel bad.
madi .... not, not to like
maestro .... teacher
magalip .... slice, to
magasgas............ wear by friction, to
magna .... walk, to
maianud .... float in, to
maibagay............ agree, to
maika-dua .... number- second
maika-tlo .... number- third
maika-uppat .... number- fourth
maikapis............ disappointed, to be
Maililiwak kenka. .... I miss you. (sing)
maipit, nalipit .... crush, to
maipulipul .... round & round, to go
mais .... plant- corn
maitibkol .... stumble, trip, stub toe, to
maitomeg............ bump head, to
maituluy .... continue, to
Maka-ananos-ak. .... I am able to be patient.
Maka-turturog-ak. .... I feel like sleeping.
maka-alis............ contagious
maka-domingo .... time- one week
makasterick............ able to enter
Maki-kuyog-ta. .... Let's go together. (sing)
Maki-trabaho-ta. .... Let's work together. (sing)
maki-idda .... lie down together, to

makigtot .... startle, to
makina .... engine, machine
malagip .... remember, to
Malak-sig iti dayta. .... Aside from that.
malammin .... body- cold, to feel
malas .... bad luck
malasin .... see, recognize, detect, to
malaylay .... plant- wilt or wither, to
malem .... time- afternoon
malipatan .... forget, to
malipit .... pinch fingers under (heavy)
mallokong .... house- bowl
malmes (lemmes) .... body- drown, to
malpas (leppas) .... finish, to (work, etc)
malsiyeb .... fingernail, to break
maminsan iti maka-bulan .... time- once a month
maminsan iti maka-domingo .... time- once a week
maminsan iti maka-tawen .... time- once a year
man .... please
manadaan .... animal- chicken, to mate
manakigayyem .... friendly
manang .... honorific, ma'am
manarnar .... bone, crushed
manen .... again
mangabak .... win, to
mangan (kaan) .... eat, to
manggagama .... insect- scorpion
manggagamud .... black magic, to practice
mangngagas .... quack doctor
mani *(Arachis hypogeia)* .... plant- peanut
mani-mani .... body- clitoris
manipud (sipud) .... from, time or place
Mano nga aldaw nga agnaedka ditoy? .... q.- How many days do you stay here?
Mano ti tawen mo? .... q.- How old are you?
Mano? .... q.- How much? How many?
manok .... animal- chicken
manong .... honorific, sir
manteka .... oil, lard
mapa .... map
mapan, in .... go, to
mapasamak .... happen, occur, to
mapattog .... spill, to
mapili .... choose, select, to
mapilit .... force, coerce, to
mapitik .... marbles, to shoot
mapunno .... fill, to
mapuyat .... stay up all night, to
mara .... prefix indicating similarity
marba (rebba), marpuog (reppoog) .... house- collapse

marigmig .... crumbs
marikna .... sense- to feel or perceive
maronggay *(Moringa oleifera)* .... tree- horseradish
Martes .... time- Tuesday
martilio .... tool- hammer
marunaw .... melt, to
marunot .... wear down, to
marurud, maassar .... angry, pissed off
masalugsug .... splinter, to get one
masapul .... need, necessary
masetas .... plants, flowering
masikog .... body fnc.- pregnant, to be
masipak .... tree- to prune branches
masisirap .... body fnc.- blind, sun
masukat .... change, relieve, replace, to
mata .... body- eyes
matay .... die, to
matchanan .... water evaporated, the rice
mateptep .... buneng, turned edge
matikapan .... body- skin, slice off a piece of
matim-og .... collide, strike, bump, to
matongpal .... promise, to break
maturog .... body fnc.- sleep, to
matutudo .... wet (rainy) season
maulaw .... dizzy, to be
mauma .... bored, weary, to be
mausar, usaren .... use, to
mauyos, masulnot, malapsut .... slip, slide, to
mayaman, nabaknang .... rich, wealthy
Maysa pay man. .... number- One more please.
maysa, una (Sp.) .... number- one
medias .... clothes- socks
medyo .... measure- half way
merienda .... snack
met .... also
mierkoles .... time- Wednesday
minartes .... time- every Tuesday
minerkoles .... time- every Wednesday
mitsa .... wick, candle
mordong .... tip or apex
moskitero .... insect- mosquito net
motorsiklo .... motorcycle
muging .... body- forehead
mukod .... body- heel (of foot)
mungay .... body- nipple

N n

naalas, na-arti, nalaad .... ugly, indecent, obscene
naalsem....... taste- sour, tart
naamo .... tame
naandor....... tough, hardy
naangdod .... body- smell, bad
naapgad ti danum .... water- salty
naapges....... body- sting, to, the skin
naarsagid .... sensitive person
naata .... ripe, not
Naawat ko ti surat mo. .... I received your letter.
nabangeg .... voice, deep
nabanglo .... smell, good, fragrant
nabangsit, naangot....... smell (stink)
nabannog .... tired, to be
nabara .... hot, red
nabartek .... drunk
nabasa....... wet
nabastos, salawasaw .... rude, impolite
nabayag....... time- a long time
Nabayag-ak nga nangan. .... time- I ate a long time ago.
nabegnat .... body- sickness return, relapse
nabistrad, nalawa .... wide
nablo (bollo)....... body- dislocated body part
naboong....... break eggs, glass
Nabsog-ak. (bussog)....... I am full. (of food)
nabual .... tree- fall at roots
nabuntog....... slow
nabunton....... pile
nadagaang....... hot, sultry, humid
nadagsen....... heavy
nadalapos....... poke straight, to
nadalison, dumalis .... wheel run over foot
nadalus .... clean
nadikket....... close, near, like friends
nagaget .... industrious
nagalis....... slippery
nagan .... name
nagango .... dried
Nagapuam?....... q.- Where have you been?
nagasang, naadat .... hot, spicy
nagasat, swerte....... good luck
nagatel, nabudo, naariek .... itchy
nagayyem....... people- friended
nagbaetan .... between
nagbukel, nagtimbukel .... round
nagbusingar, agtutot....... flow, sap
nagsabatan....... crossing, junction

naguapo, nataer, nataraki .... handsome
naibus .... no more
nailubo, nabalahoo .... mud, stuck in the
naimas........ delicious
Naimbag nga aldaw yo amin. .... Good noontime to you. (pl)
Naimbag nga bigat mo. .... Good morning to you. (sing)
Naimbag nga malem mo. .... Good afternoon to you. (sing)
Naimbag nga rabii-m. .... Good night to you. (sing)
Naimbag nga Paskua yo. .... Merry Christmas to you all.
naimbag, nasayaat, mayat........ good, well
naimut .... stingy
naingel........ taste- strong, tobacco, liquor
naingpis, nakottong........ thin
nairut........ tight, taut
naishut .... throw & hit target
nakadildillaw ti tiempo........ strange weather
nakapsut, nakapuy........ weak
nakaskasdaaw .... wonderful, surprising
nakersang........ rough
nakilnet........ consistent, chewy, firm
nakset (kesset), nasinit .... burned food
naktang .... body- muscles, sore
nakulbet........ meat, tough
nakusep........ burn bad
nakusim........ dainty eater
nalabaga........ color- red
nalabes........ excessive
nalabit .... probably, very likely
nalabudoy........ body- smooth skin
naladaw........ time- late
nalag-an .... light weight
nalagda........ durable
nalaing........ expert, efficient, capable
nalaka........ easy, cheap
nalam-ek .... cold, frigid, temperature
nalamiis........ cold, frigid, icy, water, food
nalamuyot .... smooth, soft, sleek
nalangsi, nabangles........ smell, bad (food)
nalap-it .... flexible
nalawag........ clear, light, bright
nalibeg........ water- dirty
naliday........ sad
naliknaw........ water- clean, clear
nalimpia........ no holes
nalimteg (letteg)........ swelled, puffed up
nalinis........ smooth, clean, pure
Nalipat-ak. .... I forgot.
nalisto .... time- fast, short time
nalokay........ loose

naloko .... simpleton, idiot, dolt
naloom .... ripe
nalukmeg .... fat, fleshy
nalukneng .... soft
nalumoy .... meat, tender soft
nalungtot .... rotten
nalusayat .... ripe, overripe
namaga .... dry
nana .... body- pus
nananam .... tasty, appetizing
nanang .... people- mother
nangato, ngato .... high, lofty
nangina .... expensive, dear
nangisit .... color- black
nangudel .... knife- dull
napaay .... frustrated
napait .... taste- bitter
napakil ti saka .... body- feet, tired
napalit .... viscous, thick
naparayag, agpalastog .... brag, to
napartak nga agtubo .... grows fast
napartak, napaspas, napardas .... prompt, fast, quick
napatad .... no steepness, level, equal
napateg .... precious, dear, highly esteemed
napaut .... lasting, enduring, untiring
naperde .... destroyed
napigis .... fall apart, book, clothes
napigket .... sticky
napigsa .... strong, sturdy, vigorous
napilay, lupisak, lugpi .... walk, not able to, lame
napinno .... small, fine
Napintas nga balasang! .... Beautiful girl!
Napintas ti balasang. .... She is a beautiful girl.
napintas .... beautiful, good looking
napipikel ti saka .... body- foot asleep
napitak, nalubo, nalutlut .... muddy
napudaw, puraw .... color- white
napudot .... hot, heat (weather)
napugsat .... rope break, snap
napukaw, maawan .... disappear, lose, to
napuskol .... thick, dense, heavy
narabaw, ababaw .... shallow
naraber .... good grass, new growth
Naragsak nga baru nga tawen yo. .... Happy New Year to you all.
Naragsak nga pinagbiahe-mo! .... Happy trip!
naragsak .... happy, joyous
Naragsak-ak no agkadua-ta. .... I am happy if I am with you.
narasi .... tender, soft skin, fragile
narawet .... glutton, good eater

narengngat ti daga .... cracked earth
naridem, nakudrep .... dim
narigat .... difficult
naringgor .... noisy, irritating
nariri .... noisy, say many times
narra *(Pterocarpus sp.)* .... tree- national
narubrub .... burn good
narugit .... dirty, filthy
narukop .... delicate, fragile, weak, brittle
nasadiwa .... fresh, meat, fish, etc.
nasadut .... lazy
Nasakit ti buksit ko. .... body- My stomach hurts.
Nasakit ti ulok. .... body- I have a headache.
nasakit .... sore, hurt
Nasakit ti panunot ko. .... body- My mind hurts.
nasalimuot .... body- hot, being
nasalun-at, nakaradkad .... body- healthy
nasam-it .... taste- sweet
nasamek .... weeds, tall, dense
nasanikua .... material wealth
nasapa .... time- early
nasiglat .... agile, nimble
nasikarod .... poke at an angle
nasileng .... shiny, bright
nasinggit .... voice, high
nasingpet .... virtuous, blameless, guiltless
nasipnget .... dark
nasugpet .... taste- tart, sour, acid, dry
nataba .... fatty, oily, greasy
natadem .... knife- sharp
natakrot .... timid, scared of all
natalna .... peaceful, quiet, calm
natalteg ti kalsada .... road, rough
natangken .... hard, solid, firm
natapok .... dusty
natapos .... finished, ended (month, year, etc)
natayag .... tall, high, lofty
nateng .... vegetables, generic term
natibker, nasikkil .... rigid, inflexible
natokkol .... broke, snapped, trees bones, etc
natulid, natinnag .... fall down, drop
natured .... not scared, brave, bold
naudi .... last, latest
nauyong, naunget .... angry
nawasa .... water system
nayonan .... add to
nga .... connector word
ngamin .... because
ngata .... perhaps, maybe, wonder

ngem ... but
ngilaw ... insect- house fly
ngipen ... body- teeth
ngiwat ... body- mouth
ngumato ti dalig ... wheels leave the ground
ngumisngisit nga ngumisngisit ... blacker & blacker
nisnis ... cloth, piece of, or rag
no dadduma ... time- sometimes
no kas ... as if
no kaspangarigan ... for example
no la ketdi ... provided that
no ... if
nongrona ... especially
nota ... pollen
nuang ... animal- water buffalo
nubia ... people- girl friend
numero ... number- general term

O o

oki ... body- vagina
oki-oki, longog ... valley
Okinnana! ... Damn it!
oong ... plant- mushroom
oras ... time- hour
orens ... color- orange
osoken ... pass under something, to
otong *(Vigna sinensis)* ... plant- bean, cowpea, yardlong

P p

pabatay ... stick to catch chickens
pabilo ... wick, kerosene lamp
pabo ... animal- turkey
paborita ... favorite, most desirable
Padasek ti kabaelak. ... I will try my best.
Padasem ti kabaelam. ... You try your best.
padasen ... try, attempt, to
padi ... people- father, priest
padno ... nuang- reins
pag-ong ... animal- turtle
pagampuren ... mix, to
pagarunan ... fire, place to make
pagasaan ... sharpening stone
pagay ... rice- growing
pagdagusen ... lodging place
pagigyanan ... dwelling place

pagilo	paper, toilet
pagkinorosen	carry, to (crossed items)
pagornosen	carry, to (parallel items)
pakak *(Artocarpus cummunis)*	tree- fruit, bread
pakalaglagipan	remembrance, souvenir
pakanen (kaan)	food, to give to (to feed)
pakawanen	forgive, pardon, to
Pakdaar!	Attention!
pako, sangol	nuang- yoke for
pakris	bamboo- sharp branches
palanggana	wash basin
palatang	vein, central, banana leaf
pallang *(Psophocarpus spp.)*	plant- bean, winged
pallatiwan	nuang cart- long sticks on
palsiit (lisit)	slingshot
palsuut	gun, bamboo
paltik (littik)	chalk line
paltog	gun, rifle
paltos	not really
pamarosan	plant- squash, stem
pamitik, guyodan	nuang- rope for plowing
pan-aw *(Imperata cylindrica)*	grass- cogon
panal	bird- small, grey color
panawan	dessert, to
pandek	short, in stature (people)
Pangan-anoen na?	q.- What is the use of it?
panggep	about, object, purpose
panglongboyen *(Eugenia bordenii)*	tree- good wood
panio	clothes- handkerchief
pantalon	clothes- pants, trousers
panunot	thought
Papanam?	q.- Where are you going?
papaya *(Carica papaya)*	fruit- papaya
papel	paper
para	for
paraangan	yard
paragpag	body- ribs
parda *(Dolichos ablab)*	plant- bean
parehas, isu met laeng	the same
paria *(Momordica charantia)*	plant- bittermelon
pariok	house- wok
paris	even (versus odd), equal
pasalubong	gift from the city
pasanggir	house- roof, rafter
paseeking	rattan pack
pasingsing, singat, sinsil	wedge
Pasinsiya-(ka).	I am sorry (to you).
Paskua	feast, Christmas, Easter
pasuk	stake, picket

pasuksuk .... bribe, to
paswit .... whistle, instrument
patani *(Phaseolus lunatus)* .... plant- bean, lima
patien, mamati .... believe, to
patis .... fish sauce, watery
pato .... animal- duck, white
patoke .... slide cart
paulo .... nuang- rope around horns
pay .... yet, also, more
payak .... bird- wing
payokpok .... grass- a weed
payong .... umbrella
pea .... measure- one foot
pepino .... fruit- cucumber
pfabrica .... products
pfamilia .... family
piditpidit .... body- ear, lobe of
piek .... animal- baby chick
piglat .... body- scar
pilaw .... puddle, pool of water
piliquen .... fold in half, to
pinelas, pinesat, ginapas .... grass to cut by holding it
ping-ping .... body- cheeks
pinggan .... house- plate
pinia .... fruit- pineapple
pinnakaeanak .... birthday
pinnatay .... kill, to
pirak .... silver
pisangen .... torn into pieces
pisien, iwaiwa .... cut up, to
pispis .... body- temple of head
pitaka .... wallet
pito, siete (Sp.) .... number- seven
pitsay .... fruit- bok choy
plakard .... sign
plete .... fare (for the ride)
polotan .... snack eaten w/ alcoholic drink
pongopongoan .... body- wrist
ponpon .... funeral
poon .... tree- or plant, stem or trunk of
problema .... problem, trouble
pubre .... poor, not rich
pudno .... truth
puek .... bird- owl
pugon .... charcoal pile
puligusen .... turn, nut to
puling .... body- eye, mote in the
pulos .... pure, purely
pumanakpak .... nuang- brush against something

pumanaw, agtalaw .... leave, to run away
pumugsit .... squeeze (to squirt out)
pungan .... pillow, cushion
pungdol .... tree stump
puriket *(Bidens pilosa)* .... plant- stick tights, long skinny
pusa .... animal- cat
puseg .... body- navel
pusit .... squid, dried
puso .... body- heart
putan .... tool- handle of

R r

rabanos .... fruit- radish
rabii .... time- evening, night
rabong .... bamboo- edible shoot
radyo .... radio
ragadi .... tool- hand saw
raman, ramanan .... sense- taste, to
ramay .... body- fingers
ramay nga saka .... body- toes
ramot .... plant- root of
rangtay .... bridge
rarasa .... nuang- rash from riding wet
ratik .... mildew
regalo .... gift
rekado .... ingredients
relos .... clock or watch
repetten .... bind or tie, to
repolyo .... fruit- cabbage
riari .... insect- cicada, big (male)
ridaw .... house- door
rik, kalaykay, peruya .... tool- rake
rolling, kareton .... wheeled cart
root .... weed, generic term
roskas .... nut (for bolt)
ruam, maruam .... accustom, to
rubu .... corn, ear of w/ corn removed
rumabrabii .... time- late evening
rumrumuar ti init .... time- sunrise
rumuar .... emerge, issue forth, go out, to
runo *(Miscanthus sinensis)* .... grass- bamboo
rupa .... body- face, the
rusing .... hypocotyl, seedling

S s

sa .... doubt, adverb implying
saan, haan, madi .... no
saba .... banana
Sabado .... time- Saturday
sabali .... another, other
sabon .... soap
sabung .... plant- flower
sabunganay .... banana- unopened portion of flower
Sadino?, Ayanna? .... q.- Where?
Saga bassit. .... Little by little., Slow by slow.
sagat *(Vitex parviflora)* .... tree- hardwood
sagaysan .... one by one
sagaysay .... comb
Sagmamano? .... q.- How much for one?
sagpaminsan .... seldom, rarely
sagumaymay .... house- eaves of
saka .... body- foot
sako .... sack
saksakulap .... bird- night
salaisi .... odd (versus even)
salaksak .... bird- kingfisher
salamagi *(Tamarindus indica)* .... tree- tamarind
salapi .... money- 50 cent piece
salda, abang .... rent
saleng .... tree- pine
salig *(Cordia myxa)* .... tree- palm
sallapingaw .... bird- swallow
salsalamagi .... body- lymph gland
saltek .... animal- lizard, voice of
Saludsudem, man. .... You ask, please.
salugsug .... splinter
salup .... measure- three liters
saluyot *(Corchorus olitorius)* .... plant- jute
sammisammi .... insect- beetle, green & violet
sandia .... fruit- watermelon
sang-aw .... body- breath
sanga .... lateral shoot, tine, point
sangagasut .... number- one hundred
sangal .... rope, splice
sangapulo, djis (Sp.) .... number- ten
sangapulo ket dua, dose (Sp.) .... number- twelve
sangapulo ket maysa, onse (Sp.) .... number- eleven
sangaribu .... number- one-thousand
sangio, bao .... animal- mouse, rat, shrew
sango .... front, forepart
santo, sakanto, sakbay .... before
santol *(Sandoricum koetjape)* .... tree- fruit

sao .... word, term
sapad .... banana- hand of bananas
sapasap .... common, widespread
sapatos .... clothes- shoes
Sapay la koma. .... I hope so.
saput .... insect- spider web
sara .... animal- horn, antler
sarapa .... tool- plow tooth
saringit .... branch, new
sarming .... mirror, glass
sartin .... house- dipper (for liquids)
sawi, kali .... bird- hawk
segurado .... for sure
seguru .... maybe, probably
sentro .... central, center
sentrom .... clothes- belt
sepsep .... insect- small biting fly
serraan .... close, shut, to
Siak-on! .... I'll be the one!
siam, nuebe (Sp.) .... number- nine
sida .... food, other than rice
siding .... body- mole, birthmark
Siempre. .... Certainly., Of course.
sigarilio .... cigarette
Sige ngarud. .... Okay then.
siglut .... knot
sigpit .... house- roof, cross pieces
siit .... thorn, spine, prickle, fishbone
Sika ti makaammo., Kumpormi kenka. .... The choice is yours.
Sika-on! .... You'll be the one!
siket .... body- hips
siko .... body- elbow
siksik .... scales, fish
silag *(Corypha elata)* .... tree- buri palm
silahis .... people- bisexual
silaw .... light
sili .... chili pepper
simbaan .... church
simut-simut .... insect- termite, flying stage
sinabado .... time- every Saturday
singsing .... ring (jewelry)
sinkamas *(Pachyrhizus erosus)* .... plant- bean, yambean
Sino makin kukua dayta? .... own- Who owns that?
Sino? .... q.- Who?
sinulid .... thread
sinulit, sinadut .... lazy, always
siping .... banana- growing together
sippit .... bird- beak of
sirok .... under, below

sobok .... weight
sobra .... extra
sobre ti surat .... envelope
soldado .... soldier
soli .... corner
somelia .... seedling
soso .... body- breast
soya .... soy sauce
sual .... tool- hoe, spade, straight handle
subalitan .... answer letter, to
subbual .... banana sucker
subsub .... tool- plow, digger on
subusub *(Blumea balsamifera)* .... weed- medicinal
sueldo .... salary
sugat .... body- cut, bloody
sugud-sugud *(Momordica ovata)* .... tree- rambutan
suk-suk .... shuffle cards
suka .... vinegar
sumalput .... poke through, to
sumangpet .... arrive, to
sumaruno, suroten, sumurot .... follow, to
sumayag .... axe blow, glancing, deflected
sumungbat .... answer, to
sungar .... body- goose bumps
sungrod .... fuel wood
supilyo .... toothbrush
suplian .... money- to change
supot nga pungan .... pillowcase
supot .... bag, pouch, purse
surelas .... nuang cart- cross pieces
surok .... surplus, excess, more than
sustancea .... vitamins

T t

tabako .... tobacco
tabas .... shape, fit
tabla .... board
tablon .... cant (squared timber)
tabungaw *(Lagenaria leucantha)* .... plant- squash, bottle guord
Taga-ano-(ka?) .... q.- From where (are you?)
tagapulut .... candy, sugar cane
taguab .... house- addition to
takiag .... body- upper arm
takki .... manure, dung, excrement
taktakup *(Desmodium spp.)* .... weed-
talakob .... bird trap
tali .... rope

talimpungawen .... absent minded
talipungawen .... lonely, lonesome
tallo nga daras........ time- three times
tallo pulo, triente (Sp.) .... number- thirty
tallo, tres (Sp.) .... number- three
talon .... rice field
tambak .... dam, levee, dike
tangal Viernes........ time- every Friday
tangbaw........ tool- plow shaft
tangdan .... earnings
tanggal, pupukan........ fishpond
tangkoy *(Benincasa hispida)*........ plant- squash, wax guord
tao .... people- human being
tapingar .... animal- cocks comb
tapno .... so that, in order that
taptapuyo .... insect- ant lion
taraudi .... extra, additional
tarong *(Solanum melongena)* .... plant- eggplant
tatang .... people- father, dad
tawa........ house- window
tawen........ time- year
tebbeg *(Ficus spp.)*........ tree- fruits on trunk
teltel .... body- head, back of
tengnged .... body- neck
tenidor........ house- tablefork
tenneb .... temper of metal
tiempo .... weather
tiendaan, palengke........ market
tigi *(Tacca palmata)* .... plant- edible
tilmunen .... body fnc.- swallow, to
timba........ bucket, pail
timek, uni .... body fnc.- voice
timel .... insect- flea
timid .... body- chin
tinapay........ bread
tinnawen........ time- every year
tipang .... cliff
tirad........ buneng, pencil, point of
toktok .... top of, summit
tolbek .... key
tonsan .... bottle cap
trabaho, obra........ work, job
trahe .... people- bride
tren........ train (railroad)
tsinela........ clothes- slippers, step-ins
tsleko........ clothes- sleeveless sweater
tsokolate........ color- brown
tuba........ wine- buri palm
tubbug........ sap, resin, juice

tudok ..... spit, for roasting
tugaw, bangko ..... house- bench, chair
tugi *(Dioscorea fasciculata)* ..... plant- edible tubers
tugut ..... track, footprint
tukak ..... animal- frog general name
tulang ..... body- bone
tuleng ..... body- deaf
tumagbat ..... fight, to (with buneng)
tumakder ..... stand up, to
tumakki ..... body fnc.- bowels, to move
tumalikod ..... turn around
Tumalna! ..... quiet, to be (Shut up!)
tumeng ..... body- knee
tumpaw (tapaw) ..... float, to
tumulong ..... help, to
Tumulong-ka man. ..... You help me please.
tunggal maysa ..... each & every one
turnilyo ..... bolt
turod ..... hill
tuwato ..... insect- dragon fly
tuyo ..... bran

U u

uban ..... body- hair, grey
ubbug ..... spring (water)
ubet ..... body- butt
ubi *(Dioscorea alata)* ..... plant- yam
ubing ..... people- child, baby
ugali ..... habit
ugas ..... scrubber, pot
uggot ..... leaves or shoots, young
uging, uring ..... charcoal
ugsa ..... animal- deer
ukel-ukel ..... body- testicles
uken ..... animal- puppy
ukis ..... shell, husk, peel
ukoden ..... lead, to lead by reins
uleg ..... animal- snake
ulep ..... cloud
ules ..... blanket
ulimek ..... still, silent
uliten ..... repeat, reiterate, to
ulo ..... body- head
um-uli, sumang-at ..... ascend, climb, to
uma, pagmulaan ..... farm, the (place to plant)
umabut ..... catch up with, to
umalis, umakar ..... move, change residence

umapal .... jealous, for things
umawanawan .... disappear, to
umawat .... accept, to
umay .... come, to
Umay-ka, man ditoy. .... You come here please.
umel .... body- mute
uminom .... drink, to
umisbo .... body fnc.- urinate, to
umottot .... body fnc.- fart, to
umuna .... number- first
umuneg, sumrek (serrek) .... enter, go in, to
unas *(Saccharum officinarium)* .... plant- sugar cane
unay, perme .... very, much
upa .... animal- chicken, female
uppat, kuatro (Sp.) .... number- four
urat .... body- veins
uray .... even, also
Uray ania! .... Whatever!
uray no saan .... time- never
Uray siak met. .... Even I also.
urbon .... animal- calf
urmot .... body- hair, pubic
utang .... debt, liability
utek .... body- brain

V v

vetinario .... veterinarian
Viernes .... time- Friday

W w

waig .... creek, brook
wak .... bird- crow
walis .... broom, indoor
walo, otso (Sp.) .... number- eight
wasay .... tool- ax
wasay-wasay .... insect- praying mantis
way *(Calamus spp.)* .... plant- rattan
wayway .... nuang- rope for pasturing
wen .... yes
wenna .... yes, just so
wenno .... or, lest
witiwit .... tool- plow handle

Y y

yelo .... ice
yero, galva........ house- roofing, tin
yoyo .... yoyo (a toy)

THE END

NOTES & JOURNAL

SECTION 3

Some Notes on Ilokano Culture

TABLE OF CONTENTS

INTRODUCTION

Culture Defined: An integrated system of learned behavior patterns, attitudes, and beliefs that are characteristic of the members of a particular group of people. It includes everything that a reasonably homogeneous set of people thinks, says, does, and makes, its customs, language, aesthetics, religions, material culture, and societal organization. Culture is transmitted from generation to generation.[1,2]

The international manager, to be successful in the international world of business, must be a student of culture. The ability to recognize the cultural differences between the home country and the host country is critical to success. To be able to put aside the "cultural baggage" carried along from the home country is often a necessity to being culturally sensitive. **Cultural sensitivity** may be looked upon as recognizing that the host-country culture is not going to be the same as the home culture, looking for the differences, and then acting in such a manner so that these differences will be respected. Managers must at all times remember that they are the ones who are away from home. It is their responsibility to adapt to the culture, not the responsibility of the local people to adapt to them.

---

1. Definition adapted from: **Basic Marketing - A Managerial Approach**, Mccarthy, E. Jerome and William D. Perreault, Ninth Edition, 1987, Irwin Press, Homewood, Illinois 60430, and;

2. **International Business - Introduction and Essentials**, Ball, Donald A., and Wendell H. McCulloch, Jr., Third Edition, 1988, Business Publications, Inc., Plano, Texas 75075

This paper shall examine some of the village culture that may be considered normal in the Ilokano villages of Quirino Province in the Philippines.

It should be noted well that the author does not consider himself an authority on the culture of the Ilokano people's. The following are merely observations which were made during the course of 27 months of living in the culture. In addition, these observations were made some 25 years ago (1985 – 1987) and may or may not be accurate at this time.

METHODS

The author was assigned, as a Peace Corps Volunteer (PCV), to live and work in an upland farming community as an agro-forestry specialist. His previous receipt of a Bachelor of Science degree in Forestry and 15 years experience in Forest Management made him well qualified for the position. As the only American living there, and the first American most of the younger people had ever seen, there were many stereotypical ideas about what an American "should" be like. The people expected the volunteer to be different, but the volunteer's **GOALS** were just to be a respected, active, productive member of the community. He had to be a full time student of culture as well as language to eventually be accepted into the community, as shall be seen. Just these two aspects of the job made it the challenge of a lifetime – let alone trying to accomplish anything in the field of agro-forestry.

The people "knew", from their stereotypical ideas of an American, that the volunteer should be outgoing, friendly, informal, loud, rude, extravagant, wasteful, disrespectful of elders and authority, ignorant about farming, wealthy, generous, always in a hurry, that Americans live on bread and meat and don't eat rice or vegetables, and much, much more. Of course some of these ideas are oftentimes true. The volunteer, however, had already gone through ten weeks of culture and language training in addition to training in tropical agro-forestry techniques. He had already become extremely interested and immersed in the culture while living with a Filipino host family for those 10 weeks and literally being accepted as a grandson, son, brother, and uncle in an extended family consisting of four generations. He had already become a tiny bit acculturated, so some of the stereotypical views that abounded had already been noticed and plans made to compensate for them; set answers to certain questions had already been thought through.

It would be easy, when studying with a group of Americans all day, to find oneself wanting to go out and drink a few beers with these same people in the evening, especially when the alternative is to go home to a host family and be immersed in a language that is not understandable, and in a way of life and love that is foreign to the one that a person knows and understands. The author however, was 15 – 20 years older than the typical PCV in his training group and for this reason he did not really feel at ease with these "spoiled American kids." He would therefore, go home to the host family every afternoon immediately after classes, in fact he and his host brother, who was attending university near the site where the PCV training was being held, would often accompany each other home. Another aspect of being older than average was the authors ability to recognize that two years is an extremely short time, that it generally takes a year in a new job just to become productive, and therefore he had better get started on the road to understanding what makes a Filipino tick so as to be able to be effective in his work.

RESULTS AND DISCUSSION

After the 10 weeks of training was over and the group of Volunteers was sworn in, they were sent to their work sites. The author was the only PCV within a days traveling distance of his assigned site. Here he was introduced to the real "working class" people for the first time. In this village of Luna there was a sawmill, and therefore a road. Most of the males who wanted to work could do so – either directly for the sawmill or indirectly as a maker of charcoal from sawmill waste. Both the sawmill employees and the charcoal making independent business men were earning at or above the national average GNP per capita of $630. Compared to farmers they were "well to do."

Alcohol In Community Culture

With all the money these people earned, an important factor of community culture was consumption of alcoholic beverages. The PCV did not enjoy drinking but couldn't even walk down the road at 8:00 a.m. without having people holler from their porches; "Good morning, Americano come drink with us." This was frustrating to the volunteer, who wasn't quite sure how to say "no thanks" without possibly angering somebody. It is a part of Ilokano culture that anger cannot be shown, except when one has the alibi of inebriation. People would therefore, often become belligerent and violent when drunk. This bottled up anger would and could come to the surface when people were drinking. The author was once struck by a drunken man merely for not knowing the name of the governor of a different province. The author quickly saw that it was not going to be a happy two years if this was the norm.

Religion - "Iglesia ni Cristo"

The next cultural aspect that came to the volunteers attention was religion. There is a religion in the Philippines called "Iglesia ni Cristo" which means "Church of Christ". The volunteers co-worker, an employee of the Bureau of Forest Development (BFD), was a member of this religion. One of the precepts of this religion is the fact that a person can and does buy his or her way into heaven. The volunteer was asked by his co-worker to join this church, being told that if he did jon, then the co-worker would receive 3,000 pesos credit towards heaven. The PCV politely refused, stating that he was Roman Catholic, but from that point onward there was a barrier to cooperative efforts between them. The volunteer was then sure that he was not going to be able to stay in this village for the entire two years, he already had two strikes against him in only one month.

Site Transfer

The volunteer approached his BFD supervisor, a Filipino, with thoughts about a site change. His supervisor understood perfectly, and being a Seventh Day Adventist himself, he referred to the Church of Christ as "Iglesia ni tokak" or "Church of frogs." He encouraged a site change if that was what it would take for the volunteer to be able to be effective. He assigned a different BFD technician to accompany the volunteer to another village for purposes of evaluating it as a possible new work site. The volunteers new co-worker took him to the village of Gomez. Gomez is two miles off the road, behind the mountain from Luna. On the first visit the community members of Gomez received the volunteer with open arms and enthusiasm. Gomez was (probably still is) a subsistence farming community of about 80 families spread out over 600 hectares (about 1,500 acres). At a later time the volunteer noted that "there are only two paying jobs in Gomez, the school teacher and the Peace Corps Volunteer." These people were just barely members of the cash society. They sold their excess fruit and vegetable crops at the bottom of the mountain for cash, and then immediately "traded" the cash for rice, clothing, or other necessities. On this first visit to Gomez the people butchered a dog for the PCV and made him feel welcome and wanted. They made him feel warmer, and more welcome than he had felt in his two months at Luna, where the people had never even butchered a chicken for him. The average family in Gomez earns $500 or less per year from the sale of their farm products, so the PCV anticipated no problems with alcoholics. There were, likewise no churches in the village so no problems could be foreseen in the area of religion either. The volunteer and the co-worker stayed there for two days strolling around, meeting people, and visiting their farms. After a second two day visit a week later, and the butchering of another dog, the volunteer decided to move there. The co-worker and PCV found a host family who would temporarily house the PCV, and the next week the PCV moved. Upon the recommendation of his BFD supervisor, he did not tell the people of Luna that he was leaving for good. He told them that he was being assigned to Gomez for a few weeks only.

Acceptance Into Gomez

The people of Gomez very quickly noticed that the PCV was immersed in learning the culture and language, that he was respectful of his elders, culturally sensitive, patient, and more. He had been working with his host father, a very small time logger, and his host father was impressed that he knew how to operate a chainsaw, and could even make a tree fall where he wanted it to. The host father had spread the word that the PCV appeared to be a good hard worker, and was smart too – even if he wasn't very good at speaking Ilokano. After only one month approximately 60 community members turned out to help build a small, but adequate house for the PCV. It was at this point that the real work began. The PCV was a single male living alone in his own house. His friends and neighbors asked him if he wanted a living companion. The volunteer stated that he did not. The people accepted this, but insisted that he at least take a sleeping companion. The PCV refused this offer also, but then his neighbor and good friend informed him that the people were concerned that a ghost might enter his house at night and take him over. He was also informed that the people wondered what he was trying to hide at night? Did he spend the evening counting his money or masturbating, and was that was why he was getting skinnier.

Having already accepted the fact that he had to be culturally sensitive the PCV decided that he had best do what the culture expected him to do if he was to have any luck in accomplishing his aforementioned goals. He realized that he WAS in Asia, where nobody but nobody sleeps alone, and as he had nothing to hide he told his neighbor that he would accept a sleeping companion. The neighbor said that he would talk to the other neighbors and that night they would send over two or three bachelor sons to be his companions and he could make a decision about which one of them he wanted for his permanent sleeping companion.

Sleeping Companion

As there is no electricity in Gomez people more or less live by the sun. They eat at dusk, do the dishes, sit and talk, plan for tomorrow's work, listen to the radio (when they have money for batteries), and go to sleep between 8:00 and 9:00 p.m. They then get up at 4:00 to 5:00 a.m. and start the process again. That night, shortly after supper George, Bubot, and Junior, three bachelor sons of the various neighbors, showed up at the volunteers house. The PCV was uneasy, but the boys tried to make him feel at ease. They rolled their sleeping mats out on the floor and laid down. The PCV did the same and they were all asleep shortly. Junior woke everybody up about an hour later and said; *"makibiroktayo ti balbalasang,"* or "let's go search for girls." The other 3 declined and sent Junior to satisfy his needs. He came back and woke everybody up again later on trying to convince the others to go with him. They declined the invitation again and Junior left. The next morning George and Bubot stayed long enough to be sure that the volunteer knew how to get his charcoal lit, use his charcoal stove, and cook his rice, then they left. That day the PCV told his neighbor that he didn't want Junior to come again, but that George and Bubot were welcome to return.

That night, and for the next several nights, George and Bubot returned to the PCV's house to sleep. The PCV began to feel more at ease with them, but noticed that Bubot would ask questions every night about how much the PCV's radio and other belongings had cost in America, and if he could have them when the PCV went home. By the end of a week Bubot had asked the PCV the cost of everything that he owned, and he also wanted it all when the volunteer left to return to America. George, on the other hand, was more shy and reserved. He never asked if he could have anything, was mannerly, polite, never laughed at the PCV's fledgling Ilokano, and respected him as an elder is supposed to be respected. Only 5 or 6 people in the entire village had ever been beyond 4th grade in school, and for this reason there was absolutely no English spoken at all, other than numbers. The PCV had to become proficient at Ilokano to be able to converse, and understand what was going on around him. George was very helpful in this respect, while Bubot would spend half of the evening laughing at the PCV's efforts.

After about two weeks the novelty apparently wore off for Bubot, or maybe George said something to him, regardless he stopped coming to the PCV's house. George and the PCV however, became the best of faithful friends, and George slept at the PCV's house virtually every night for the remaining 21 months that the volunteer lived in Gomez.

The Grapevine

The PCV noticed that the village grapevine worked very effectively and that the stories he told George were quickly known around the village. It also quickly became apparent that George was selective in what he passed on to the grapevine. He respected the PCV's personal life and did not pass on things that might hurt the volunteers credibility – for instance, George never passed on the fact that the PCV knew virtually nothing about growing corn. As these stories passed through the grapevine people began to have more respect for the volunteer, and the PCV gave George the primary credit for his eventual acceptance into the community. The volunteers credibility grew and grew as time progressed, as shall be seen.

The Necessity Of Demonstration

The peoples farms were, for the most part, a mile up the mountain from their houses for the reason that actual stewardship of the land was given to them after the fact. This shall not be gone into in greater detail. Because the farms were far away from the house, if the family did not go to the farm on a given day they had nothing to eat except rice and salt. The expense of meat forced the people to live nearly exclusively on fruits and vegetables, and of course rice. A meal that had meat in it was considered something special. The people raised chickens and about once a month they would butcher one.

The PCV started out by demonstrating how to grow a beautiful back yard garden. In training he had learned of a gardening technique called F.A.I.T.H., an acronym for Food Always In The Home. He had enthusiasm for it and after two months of just telling people about it he came to the conclusion that another aspect of Lesser Developed Country (LDC) culture is that people have to be shown that something is truly better before they will be convinced to try it. They are not going to take anybody's word for anything – after all, this is the way their ancestors did it – so it must be right. The PCV, therefore, obtained some help to clear approximately a 10 meter by 15 meter patch of abandoned, sterile ground near his home, and he planted a FAITH garden. Within two months he was harvesting more fresh vegetables than he could eat and was giving the excess to George's family. The PCV was also being culturally sensitive in another respect, and had switched to a diet of fruits, vegetables and rice for all three meals a day, seven days a week. People came from far away and viewed the PCV's garden with amazement. With just this little piece of land he was getting all this food, and it seemed to be just because he had put all that old dead grass (mulch) on the ground. The PCV told the people that when the old dead grass rotted it would make fertilizer. Before anybody else tried FAITH gardening the soil had improved enough so that it supported a good population of earthworms again and the neighbors pigs became a problem because of this. The favorite food of pigs is earthworms, the PCV was told, and therefore the more earthworms there are, the more problems there would be with pigs. The people refused to tie up or pen their pigs, so the PCV requested George and his fathers help to fence his garden. They built a fence of split bamboo – which endured only about two

George Hauling Charcoal to Market

months before the pigs broke it down. By the end of approximately 6 months the PCV had given up in the battle against the pigs, and the FAITH garden was abandoned. This brings to light a strange cultural aspect. The people would rather let their pigs run loose and eat good than be able to eat good themselves. By tying or penning their pigs and bringing them food, they could have grown the most beautiful gardens imaginable, but they would rather let their pigs roam free. People who lived far from pigs had already begun FAITH gardening and all in all the PCV could see no big advantage in attempting to fight the pigs. It was extremely frustrating to see a beautiful garden destroyed as regular as clockwork by them. It didn't matter, as the seed was growing in the PCV's mind to demonstrate something larger, something that would have longer range effects, and truly be an accomplishment that he could be proud of.

The First Year Draws To A Close

At this point the first year was drawing to a close. The PCV had learned a lot about culture, beliefs, customs, and folklore as well as the language of the Ilokano people. In addition to learning that people had to be shown that a new process of doing something made sense before they would try it he had also learned the cultural aspects of birthdays, Christmas, weddings, anger between two people, and much more. Some of these cultural aspects shall now be addressed before progressing on to the second year.

Birthdays

An Ilokano birthday celebration, unlike an American one, where the guests bring presents for the person who is celebrating, contrasts in the respect that the Ilokano birthday celebration sees the person who is having the birthday, if he or she invites friends for the birthday celebration, cooking a big meal of special foods and feeding all the guests. There will however, be no gift giving. People don't have money to be able to give presents, they never have had, and therefore a birthday isn't even considered a time to give gifts.

Christmas

Christmas, on the other hand, is considered a time to give gifts, but unlike the USA where many people seem to forget the true meaning of Christmas and see it as a time to clean up in the presents department, the Ilokano looks upon Christmas as a day to relax, eat special food, celebrate as a community and as a family, and have a happy time. Any presents exchanged are fairly inconsequential, but important and special to the person receiving them. A typical present may be a bar of soap, a pair of fingernail clippers, a small mirror, or a towel. Christmas was a very special time to the PCV as it showed him how close George and he had actually become. For Christmas, George gave the PCV a whole cooked chicken, and the PCV gave George a T-shirt with a design on it. The PCV was extremely moved by George's present to him. He knew that the family itself could only butcher about one chicken a month for its own use, so although small, the PCV looked upon this gift as a gift of a month's supply of meat. He hugged George so tight that he practically broke his ribs.

Opening Presents

Another Ilokano aspect of gift giving is that the receiver does not open a gift in the presence of the giver. The giver knows that whatever present he or she has given is small and inconsequential, so the receiver is not expected to open it in the presence of the giver and embarrass him. The receiver of the gift will only open it after the giver has left. The PCV had learned this from George. Whenever the volunteer had to be gone from Gomez for a Peace Corps meeting, seminar, or training he would ask George to watch his house and guard his garden from the pigs, and upon his return he would always bring George some small present, usually a pair of short pants. Shorts or short pants (similar to an American swim-suit) were the normal work garb and as such were a high demand item. The first time the PCV brought George a "thank you for guarding the house present" and gave it to George that night when he came to the PCV's house to sleep, George politely thanked the PCV and placed the newspaper wrapped package in the corner. The PCV asked George why he didn't open it and he obligingly explained. The PCV explained the custom in America and asked George to please open the package because the PCV wanted to see his smile. George obliged and opened the package, and he was thrilled. He told the PCV that he didn't have to bring him anything just for guarding his house and garden, especially because the pigs had broken through the fence again and destroyed a whole row of okra. The PCV made it a habit however, to bring back a pair of short pants or a T-shirt for George every time he had to be gone for a few days. After that first time George would always hold the package a minute and look at the PCV with eyes that questioned "Should I open it?" The PCV would merely shake his head yes and George would open it. This was one area in which, because of their friendship, the PCV did not have to strictly follow the cultural norm.

Weddings

The wedding celebration is substantially different from what we are familiar with in the United States. The PCV only attended two weddings, that was all he wanted to attend. To him they were long and boring. Everybody in the village is automatically invited, by word of mouth, to all weddings. The PCV went to the first two that he was invited to, primarily out of a sense of obligation to the inviter. A wedding party starts about 8:00 p.m., outdoors, after about 30 – 50 people have arrived. The village members have rented a battery powered record player with HUGE speakers and about 6 – 10 45-RPM records. The single girls (balasang) sit on benches on one side of the dirt "dance floor" and the bachelors (baru) mill around in the crowd. This is where the young men meet the girl that they will eventually marry. If the author may be allowed to leave the wedding party momentarily to present another point of interest that is appropriate at this time: there is no dating as such, no mixing of the sexes in normal day to day activities. The bachelors and balasangs will never mix in other places. Aside from wedding parties the only way a bachelor can see a girl that he likes is to ask a minimum of two friends to go with him to her home. There they will sit in a group with the family of the girl and converse until maybe 9 or 10:00 p.m., and then go home; a late night! The chances are slim that a bachelor has ever been alone with his bride until after the wedding.

For this reason wedding parties are important events where a bachelor and a balasang can actually be close and even touch! Despite the fact that a young man may be particularly attracted to a certain girl, he is expected to divide his dances between all the girls.

It would look very bad and be the talk of the village if a bachelor danced with the same balasang more than about 5 times during the night.

Back to the wedding party: The battery powered phonograph is playing the same 6 – 10 45-RPM records over and over at about 100 decibels, and the bachelors can pay "the master of the phonograph" to play a special request, from the very limited selection of records. This raises money for the bride and groom. The dancing goes on until dawn and then most people go home. The bride and groom go to a church, with a few INVITED people, and a priest joins the two together as husband and wife. They return home, and by then anybody who wants to, is waiting at their house to congratulate them. About noon some pigs and/or goats and/or dogs will be butchered by the guests. These may be donated by other village members, but if not then the groom is expected to furnish them. There must be enough food to satisfy the hunger of however many guests may show up. If there were to be a shortage of food on the wedding day, then it would be a bad omen indicating that food would be in short supply during the couples entire married life. This day is merely for storytelling and such. The bachelors and balasangs have all gone home and this part of the wedding party is for the adults. About 4 – 5:00 p.m. the crowd eats and soon disperses, to be able to be home before dark. The bride and groom finally get to relax and be alone for the first time. All the cleaning up of the food and so on has been done by the guests. The volunteer could easily visualize the bride and groom breathing a sigh of relief and falling asleep in each other's arms, that is, if they weren't too shy this first night.

Death

Death is treated very differently than in America. The traditional Ilokano wake always seemed extremely rude to the PCV. He saw entirely too many deaths and wakes in his two year stay. People died regularly, more children than older people. This was the reason the wake seemed extremely insensitive to the PCV. A child would die of something like measles or chicken pox because the parents did not have the money to go to a doctor. Then they would have to beg, borrow, or steal enough money to be able to feed all the people who would come to their house for the next nine nights for the wake.

The first thing that happened after a death was that all the men who had either hand tools or skills would go to the house of the dead and build a coffin. This would generally be early morning as the child would die during the night, and word would spread very rapidly through the grapevine. This would be a time of solemnity and sadness. There would be very little talking among the coffin builders. People would come and go during the day, friends offering condolences, helping in whatever ways they could. That night, anybody who wanted to, was welcome to come over for the first night of the wake. Those who could afford to do so would bring a chicken. Before the night was over there would be a feed for all the people who were present. It would have been considered rude however, to bring fruits, vegetables, or other farm crops. This would have implied that the family wasn't good enough farmers to have enough of those foods. This first night was quite solemn, the body was still in the house, and one should not be rude or noisy. There were certain nights when bachelors could come and certain other nights when the balasangs could come. A wake was not considered a time when a boy and girl should meet or court. The single people would go home at about 10 p.m. to midnight and the adults that remained would play cards and converse until dawn. That day the burial would take place. Pallbearers would have been selected during the night, and they would carry the coffin on their shoulders to the cemetery, which was about 5 miles from Gomez. They would perform the burial, generally marking the grave with a simple wooden cross, and then go home.

The second night the wake would be more joyful. There would be no music for a wake but there would be games and other diversions to keep people awake. The ghost was now roaming about the village trying to figure out where to go, what to do, what had happened. If the person had not been ready to die, and was not given a happy send off into the next world, it could make problems for another person by entering their body and causing bad luck or medical problems. Unexplainable stomach problems were often blamed on ghosts.

For nine nights this would continue. Every night the family of the dead would have to feed all the people who came. Because of the fact that the ghost was now roaming around, certain precautions also had to be taken at night while sleeping. People slept as far away as possible from any openings in the house, and on these nights of the wake, they also took particular care to make sure that they were in tight body contact with each other all night. If the ghost entered the house at all, it was a sightless thing and hopefully couldn't find anybody. If it did bump into the sleeping mass of people, it couldn't differentiate one from the other and therefore couldn't enter into any single one of them. The PCV, when told by George that this was the reason he wanted to sleep legs and arms all intertwined, again showed cultural sensitivity by agreeing to it. This would go on all nine nights of the wake, and then George would once again be happy to sleep with just shoulders or hips touching. This cultural aspect shall be addressed after completion of the death culture.

The ninth night of the wake was the grand finale, so to speak. This was the night that the ghost would be given its final send-off. It was a night of special activities. There would be games for even the smallest children. There was supposed to be ample joy and laughter this night. The family of the deceased one would also prepare special foods this night, and more people would come than any other night. The younger people would stay until about midnight, and the remainder of the night the older men and women would talk, party, play cards, eat, drink, and generally attempt to be merry. At dawn everybody would again go home, and that was the official end of the wake.

An American visitor to the PCV's village once noted that "they don't grieve like we do, they have so many children that death is no problem and they don't truly grieve". The PCV wants to emphasize that this is absolutely not true. They grieve as much as any American person who loses a son or daughter, mother or father, grandmother or grandfather.

The Culture Of Sleeping

The sleeping practices of the people were also noted to be different than in the United States. More cultural baggage that the PCV had to stow away until his return home. In America people who aren't married, be they brothers or friends, will generally feel funny sleeping together, especially two males. Children in America are generally given their own bedrooms when they become old enough so that they may feel a need or want for privacy. When they are forced to sleep together later in life two males will spend the entire night making sure that they have several inches of space between them. Ilokano, and Philippine culture in general, has mats spread out on the floor of the largest room of the house and everybody sleeps shoulder to shoulder, hip to hip. What your older brother next to you, or your father and mother are doing is none of your concern. It can be said however, that this, plus watching the chickens, dogs, pigs, and water buffaloes; made a youngster cognizant of the facts of life at a very young age. Young people were wise and mature in this respect and in many other respects, when compared to American youngsters. American youngsters will generally be found snickering about sexual connotations even when they are 16 years old, while the Filipino youngster will stop this immature action when he or she is about 10 years old.

The PCV had learned of this sleeping practice while living with the host family during his ten weeks of training, so he wasn't surprised, didn't think it out of the ordinary when Junior, Bubot, and George sandwiched him between them that very first night that they all slept together. As George and the PCV became closer friends the PCV came to like sleeping in contact with his friend. It gave him a sense of security, and seemed to make life in a strange land just a little bit less difficult.

Time References

The PCV noted very distinct differences in the time references between Filipinos and Americans. Americans are generally taught to be prompt. The PCV had noticed that the Filipino was generally at least an hour late to any meeting that he might call. After he gave George an old watch – that still worked well – he noticed one day that when he asked George what time it was that George looked at his watch – a digital readout – and although it said 10:59 a.m., George responded that "It is still only ten o'clock." "Ah-ha," thought the PCV, "that must be why everybody is always an hour late for meetings." He'd also noticed a cultural difference in respect to longer time periods. Most people thought no further ahead than to the next harvest. There was no thought about how to get ahead, or make life easier for oneself in the long run. For this reason the PCV had a difficult time convincing people to plant trees, such as citrus trees. They wouldn't, after all, bear fruit for 4 – 7 years! That's longer than forever to a farmer who only has concerns and worries for a time period no longer than 4 months in the future, a 10th to a 20th of the time that it will take an orange or mandarin tree to bear fruit.

People didn't, however, seem to have the habit of putting off until tomorrow, what could be done today. These farmers were (generally) probably the hardest working, most industrious people that the volunteer had ever seen. They usually worked on their farms six days a week, and then used Sunday to relax and plan for the upcoming week.

Anger

The most enlightening experience the PCV had with anger was when he discovered that if two people were angry with each other, it took a go-between or intermediary to patch up the differences. The PCV saw this in action once while living with the host family during training. His host father and 18 year old host brother exchanged words in anger, and for two days after that the father and son would not be seen in the same room together, while the mother acted as intermediary to patch up their differences. The

PCV was even drawn into it when his host mother asked him to tell his host brother that he should respect his father, and why. She informed the PCV that his host brother would surely listen to him.

The volunteer was drawn into the very center of an argument by being expected to play the part of the intermediary after George and his father had an argument in Gomez and George left home for four days. George had gone 40 kilometers away, to the home of his Aunt and Uncle in another village. The PCV had the opportunity to go and try to act as the intermediary between George and his father. He received specific instructions from George's parents about what to say when he found George, and off he went, to attempt to convince George that he should come home. He was proud that he succeeded in this attempt, and to everybody's relief George did come home. For a more complete description of this event see attached, Appendix A.[3.]

Going Into The Second Year

As stated above, a seed had been growing in the PCV's mind for a larger demonstration. He had noticed and been frustrated ever

---

3. Appendix A , by the author, was published in ***Salaysayan - Peace Corps Philippines***, October 1987.

since his arrival in Gomez, by the farmer's normal practice of plowing up and down the slopes versus across the slopes. He had noticed the deep erosion gullies that resulted from this practice, as the rains were funneled straight down the mountains. The people didn't like the fact that if it rained immediately after planting, half of their corn seed ended up in the streams at the base of the mountain, but they didn't seem to know what to do about it. The PCV had stressed contour plowing in virtually every meeting of the farmers association that he had addressed. He had talked to George about the problem and George had explained that the reason the people plowed up and down the mountain was because that was the way it had been done forever, that the water buffalo did not like pulling the plow across the hillside, that no, he'd never tried plowing across the hillside; his father had told him how to plow, so he did it. The PCV wanted to change this practice before his time was up. He had established credibility for himself, was a highly respected member of the community, was considered an industrious person with a great deal of patience, and much more, and thought he could accomplish this new task he set for himself.

His thought was to purchase a water buffalo and do a full blown demonstration farm. He presented the idea to George, who thought it was a good idea and told his father about it. George's father talked to the PCV, and offered to let him use a part of their farm for whatever he wanted to do. The PCV was somewhat apprehensive about the thoughts of purchasing a water buffalo as he didn't know the first thing about raising a large animal. He therefore discussed it at length with George. It was their topic of conversation for several nights. The PCV had to be sure that George would show him all that he had to know about the "care and feeding of water buffalo", that he would show him how to farm, and that they could help each other on their farms. He wanted to be absolutely sure that George wasn't just saying what he knew the PCV wanted to hear. After about two weeks of talking and being reassured by George, the PCV made the decision to go ahead. George's father offered to help the PCV find and purchase a water buffalo. He told the PCV that he could expect to pay about 5,000 to 8,000 pesos ($250 – $400) for a water buffalo. They searched far and wide, and every place they went the sellers wanted 10,000 pesos as soon as they discovered that it was the Americano who was doing the buying. George's father came up with the plan of telling the next seller that they were buying the water buffalo for him, not for the Americano, and in that way they could find one that the PCV could afford. Using this trick they found a 12 year old female (a strong, healthy animal in the prime of life) for the price of 6,000 pesos ($300). The PCV bought it, and George, true to his word, showed him how and where to pasture it, when, where and how to bathe it, when to make sure it was in the shade, and so on for the first few days. The PCV had already ridden George's water buffalo enough so that he would no longer fall off and land on his head, so George just had to keep a loose eye on him. Water buffalo are extremely smart, and a well trained one will respond to several voice commands as well as rope (non-verbal) commands. The PCV purchased his water buffalo in October, right at the start of the fall plowing/planting season. His plan was to plow his farm on the contour, thereby showing people that a water buffalo could walk and plow on the contour just as easily, in fact, as it could pull a plow up and down the mountain. With the help of several friends the eight foot tall cogon grass was removed from the area where the PCV was to farm, he found a plow that the owner happily traded for a $5 solar powered calculator, and George taught him how to plow with a water buffalo. He plowed his farm on the contour, and immediately George requested and received his fathers permission to plow his farm on the contour also. There were a few other people who had not yet plowed their farms, and when these people saw that it was possible for the water buffalo to work on the contour they followed the example of the PCV and his friend George. Over the course of the growing season everybody who had plowed on the contour noticed that their farms did not develop erosion gullies, and that none of their seed ended up in the streams at the bottom of the mountain.

The PCV felt elated at this easy success. The next planting season only one die-hard farmer continued plowing/planting up and down the slope. The results of this ended up being a very dramatic demonstration of the benefits of contour plowing. About two days after the completion of planting there was a real gully-washer of a rain storm, and the one farmer who had plowed up and down the slope was wiped out, virtually all of his corn seed had ended up at the bottom of the mountain. The people who had plowed on the contour were very quick to note that they had lost none of their seed.

That next planting season the PCV introduced hybrid corn to George. He bought one kilogram of this seed in town and gave it to George to plant on a corner of his farm. He traded George some of his home grown seed for the hybrid corn, pointing out to George that this was "special" corn seed, and that he wanted George to plant it on his farm and watch it in comparison to his other corn, as the soil on his farm was better than the soil on the PCV's farm. George, and for that matter most of the people were by now willing to place some little bit of faith and trust in what the PCV was saying, so George did not hesitate to accept and plant the hybrid seed. The PCV likewise, informed George that he should not save the seed from this corn, that the next year it would be smaller and less healthy than this year. It was difficult to explain why this was so, that hybrid crops tend to revert back to the characteristics of a single parent if saved and planted again. Maybe George didn't understand, but he was intelligent enough to realize that there was a good reason why he should not save and plant the seed obtained from the hybrid corn. He and his family were highly impressed by the results of the hybrid corn, and stated that it was worth the extra expense of purchasing this special seed over saving their own and that next planting season they would plant all hybrid corn seed. The PCV's credibility and spirits again soared with this latest success. His credibility had been rising rapidly ever since his first demonstration of FAITH gardening. It leveled off for a time period, and then when he bought the water buffalo his credibility again increased rapidly.

Owning A Water Buffalo (Nuang)

After the PCV bought the water buffalo (**nuang**) the people of Gomez were rather amazed. They knew that he was industrious and more but they never expected him to see him riding and using his own nuang! As he became proficient at riding the creature, using it to plow his farm, helping George by using it to pull carts of bananas down the mountain, and so on, the people actually became proud of "their Americano." The PCV soon noticed that when he would make his weekly trip to the public market, 10 kilometers and 2 hours away, people that he didn't even know would make comments to him about his nuang. He knew that the only way these strangers could know was because the people of Gomez had told them. It was soon known far and wide that "the Peace Corps at Gomez owns a nuang."

After owning his nuang about one month, there was a Sunday afternoon when it was grazing around George's yard, and George's bull nuang hopped on and mated with the PCV's nuang. George and his family were impressed, and told the volunteer that he was very lucky. He asked them how long it would be before she would calf. The people, no matter who he asked, said that it took the same nine months that it took for people. The PCV had a book that said the gestation period of water buffalo was 320 days, or about ten and one-half months. The people insisted that the book was not correct, that it was 9 months. After nine months came and went and there was no calf, but the nuang was obviously pregnant, the people said maybe it would be 10 months. It ended up being 315 days. The PCV had taught the people something else that they had never been sure of. The PCV only had one month remaining in his service after his nuang calved, but noted that within that last

Author's Water Buffalo (Nuang) and four hour old calf

month, two different families had come to him with the date their water buffalo was serviced, and they asked the PCV when she would calf.

After the volunteers nuang became pregnant his credibility seemed to go up even further. The people seemed to think that he had planned for her to become pregnant so that he could see a new calf before he went home. Water buffalo do not become pregnant often, as the cow has a silent heat, and the only one who knows she is in heat is the bull. As peoples nuangs are generally used on the farm all day and tied up when they aren't actually being used, there is little opportunity for a bull and cow to come together during the

The author bathing his Water Buffalo (Nuang)

18 – 24 hour estrous cycle. Even George, in his 18 years, had never seen a newborn nuang calf, and had no real idea how long the gestation period was. In his two years the PCV only saw two calves – his own and one other. Then when the volunteers nuang actually calved the people were truly impressed. It was unfortunate that the PCV only had one month to go. The peoples respect for him and his credibility was so high at this point that they might have even been able to be talked into planting some citrus fruit trees, as George had already done.

On Being Gay

The PCV had read some materials while in training which informed him that although gayness is generally accepted by Filipino people, that one should not make a big point of the fact that "I am gay", at least not at the start. The PCV did happen to be gay and although he never came right out and told anybody, they eventually deduced it from the way he lived, acted, carried himself and even sat while relaxing. Of course after a while George knew of the PCV's desires and tendencies, but this is one of the personal things which he never spread through the grapevine. The materials which the PCV had read in training indicated that one should do everything possible to establish the fact that he or she was a hard-worker, responsible, culturally sensitive and so on before allowing anybody to know that he or she is gay. Eventually the PCV heard people talking about his gayness, but they never looked down upon him or made any comments or criticisms about it. The PCV learned that one young male who was very obviously gay had deduced that the PCV was gay and had spread the word. For a few days it was the talk of the village, but nobody ever made any derogatory comments to the PCV and he also never noticed any difference in the way people treated him after they learned of his gayness.

A Filipino male child who is too interested in cleaning the house, making flower bouquets, washing the dishes or generally hanging around mother's apron strings is assumed to have gay tendencies and will be treated as such. It is no problem. They accept the boy without question (the author has no experience or knowledge with/of female gayness in Philippine culture). It should also be noted that if a male sits with his legs crossed that people may assume that one is gay. A child once asked the PCV if he was bakla (gay) just because he was sitting with his legs crossed.

There are also gay barbers. You can identify a gay barber because he has a nicer barber shop than the straight barber and while he is giving you a haircut he will tend to rub against you more than is called for. If a person doesn't like gay people then it's best to be culturally sensitive and just keep quiet and not go to that barber again in the future.

CONCLUSION

The above illustrations have, hopefully, been enlightening to the reader in showing that there are very definite cultural differences between the peoples of different countries, and that these differences must be respected by practicing cultural sensitivity. It is only by practicing this cultural sensitivity in everyday life, that a manager can hope to gain the respect of the people, to gain some credibility, and be able to accomplish what he or she is trying to do. Once the people realize that a person is doing his or her best to be culturally sensitive, that he or she is genuinely interested in and doing his or her best to show respect for their culture, then they will be willing to help the person in whatever ways they can to adjust to their society and its culture. The cultural differences illustrated above are just a few that the author noted in his two years as a Peace Corps Volunteer.

APPENDIX A

From Salaysayan Magazine

Peace Corps Philippines

October 1987

A RICH AND RARE EXPERIENCE

Story by Daniel Wieczorek

What is involvement? The dictionary gives several meanings, but I think my definition would be "to become a part of or to have something become a part of you."

A fellow PCV once commented to me, "I really feel that if you cling too tightly to other volunteers, you'll never have a really satisfying experience here…". I responded, "I feel that how close you get to your Filipino brothers and sisters will determine, in the long run, how good/satisfying/fulfilling your Peace Corps experience is." Once at my site, I developed some close personal friendships, one in particular – maybe because we both put so much mental energy into developing it.

Over the course of a week, I realized just how important and close that one friend is, and how deeply involved I am with his family. If I don't accomplish anything more than what I did that one week, I can still say that my Peace Corps experience has been richly rewarding and fulfilling – for I had the rare opportunity to bring a family back together.

As soon as I moved into my own house, friends and neighbors asked if I wanted a companion. I said no, as most volunteers do, but it quickly became obvious that the people felt I was trying to hide something. Plus, they were genuinely worried about me because of the ghosts in the area! I thought, "Well, this *is* Asia, where nobody but nobody sleeps alone, and since I have nothing to hide, I could have somebody spend the nights with me." I chose my neighbor's 17-year-old son George as my permanent sleeping companion. He was mannerly, polite, laughed at my fledgling Ilocano the least and was the least concerned about how much my belongings cost and would I give them to him when I went home. I'm old enough to be George's father, but we've become closer than me and my real brother back in America.

I quickly came to enjoy and value George's presence every night. He never fails to call me Manong, or older brother. In this mountain barrio of Gomez, Cabarroguis, Quirino, there are no sari-sari stores, no place to go have a drink or eat ice cream; there isn't even electricity. Life virtually comes to a halt at dark. Without George, there would be nothing to do except read a book or write a letter by kerosene light, further destroying my eyes.

George, upon his arrival each evening, sweeps the floor, closes the windows, rolls out the sleeping mats, and we talk. In pure Ilocano, he tells me what he did that day. With a fourth grade education, George knows English colors and numbers and that's about the extent of it. We converse with lots of examples, drawings on the floor or in the air, and searching my Ilocano dictionary. George is highly motivated to have the most productive bankag, or vegetable farm, on the mountain so his daily stories are always interesting and informative. When he finishes, I tell him what I did during the day and ask him the Ilocano for some new weed, fruit tree or insect that I've dragged home that day. If it's still early, I'll tell stories about life in Alaska or life in America in general. No matter how twisted my Ilocano is, he never laughs at me; he only tries to understand, then tells me how to say it more beautifully. About 8 p.m. we go to sleep and like a clock, George always wakes up within 10 minutes of 5 a.m. We roll up the sleeping mats, fold the blankets, put it all on the shelf and he leaves.

One Tuesday, I was to help George on his farm-weeding the area where he had planted 60 mandarin trees. But when I went to his house, his father looked angry and then his mother began crying. His father told me George had "left home." He explained what had happened, but all I really understood was that George and his father had argued and when his father told him to leave – meaning to go to the farm – George packed his bag and left. I ran down the mountain and caught George as he passed in a jeepney. We had a good talk but no matter what I said, he insisted there was no problem and he was only going to visit his aunt and uncle in Escoting for a few days. Then he was off on the next jeepney.

I slowly and sorrowfully climbed back up the mountain. I told his mother and father about our conversation, we all cried, and his father told me that his anger is very fast to disappear and that even now he was no longer angry. He said he didn't think George would return in a few days because he would be afraid. I offered to go to Escoting if George didn't return on Friday, and his parents were quite happy that I would consider acting as the go-between. So, for three days we all cried and worried a lot, and I got to know that family in a much deeper way than I had previously known them.

Every night I put George's sleeping mat, pillow and blanket on the floor as if he was going to return moment. I believe in ESP any moment. I believe in ESP and mind-to-mind communication, so I assumed George would know somewhere inside him that I was ready for his return and he'd also know I'd be coming to get him on Saturday.

George didn't return on Friday so I headed for Escoting in a downpour. After an hour's walk down our mountain, an hour's jeepney ride and another hour's walk into Escoting, I arrived. Upon finding George, I asked when he was returning, and he answered, "Not for a long time." We went where we were able to talk uninterrupted and I delivered messages from his father, mother and friends in Gomez, and told him of my own personal sadness. By the time I was done, we were both crying, and when I asked again when he was coming home, he said, "Tomorrow." Since he had left alone, he wanted to return alone, so I would go ahead and he'd be home about noon on Sunday.

I arrived back home in Gomez at dusk, sore-footed after walking barefoot in the mud for 15 kilometers. When I talked to George's parents, they were very happy and relieved.

Back at my house, I ate a good supper for the first time in four days and slept well for the first time in four nights, secure in the knowledge of what I had accomplished. Sunday morning, I cleaned house, did laundry then WAITED. At 11 :37 a.m., George's father hollered my name and said George had arrived. I ran to their house and saw the happiest group of faces I think I've ever seen in my life. George and I shook hands and I thanked him, but then left so they could be alone as a family. By and by, George came to my house. I asked if he was happy to be home and even before he answered "Wen (yes), Manong," I knew by the smile that stretched from ear to ear that he was as happy as any 17-year-old could be. What an incredibly warm feeling for me!

When he came that night to sleep, we both had long stories to tell. One thing I asked him was if he knew somehow that I would be coming to Escoting for him. He answered, "Yes, I knew you would come."

THE END

Made in the USA
Middletown, DE
14 October 2022

12759400R00086